ART ISRAEL

26 PAINTERS AND SCULPTORS

by William C. Seitz

An exhibition organized by The Museum of Modern Art, under the

joint auspices of the America-Israel Cultural Foundation, Inc. and

the International Council of The Museum of Modern Art, New York

THE MUSEUM OF MODERN ART, NEW YORK

Distributed by Doubleday & Co., Inc., Garden City, New York

An art exhibition can serve as a cultural ambassador, revealing a nation's soul. It is our sincere hope that *Art Israel: 26 Painters and Sculptors* will sustain this role.

It is part of Israel's day-to-day creativity, and is a reflection through art of her spiritual and cultural life. This exhibition serves another purpose, too— that of educating our own people toward beauty in this old, new land—a country which, despite its association with the Bible, is not primarily exotic nor extraordinary, but simple: striving at what others accomplished long ago.

We hope this exhibition may be a signpost to the flowering of art in our country, and we offer it to you as a crystallization of aspects of cultural life in modern Israel.

LEVI ESHKOL
Prime Minister of Israel

The America-Israel Cultural Foundation, which dedicates itself to the furtherance of cultural life in Israel, is proud to co-sponsor, with the International Council of The Museum of Modern Art, New York, this exhibition reflecting the work of Israel's contemporary painters and sculptors.

When Israel became independent in 1948, it was clear that all available resources had to be used to build the economy of a new nation if it were to survive. This meant that cultural life and institutions would suffer unless help was forthcoming. To a people who have an irrepressible hunger for all the arts, any curtailment of cultural activities during those difficult days would have caused indescribable hardship.

Recognizing this, the Israeli government turned to the America-Israel Cultural Foundation, which was then, and still remains, the major organization in the United States aiding Israel's cultural life. Its program has included supporting cultural projects in Israel, encouraging her gifted young people through scholarship programs, and bringing to the United States such groups as the Israel Philharmonic Orchestra, Habimah, and Inbal. We hope that the work of the painters and sculptors represented in the *Art Israel* exhibition will demonstrate that in art, as well as in music, theater, and dance, Israel can make a durable contribution to the enrichment of all our lives.

We wish to extend our appreciation to the Art Committee of the Foundation's Women's Division, to Dr. William C. Seitz, Associate Curator, Department of Painting and Sculpture Exhibitions, The Museum of Modern Art, for his patience and enthusiasm in selecting the exhibition, and to the Jewish Museum for its hospitality in presenting the inaugural showing. We are particularly grateful to the International Council of The Museum of Modern Art, under whose auspices this first major Israeli art exhibition will be circulated to fifteen institutions in the United States and Canada over the next two years.

WILLIAM MAZER
Chairman of the Board,
America-Israel Cultural Foundation, Inc.

The twenty-six artists presented in this exhibition make up a cross section of Israeli art today. They were selected only after the work of more than seven hundred artists had been viewed in New York, Paris, and London, as well as in studios, galleries, exhibitions, and kibbutzim throughout Israel. Some were famous at home and known outside; others were all but unknown even in their own country. Certain artists very popular in Israel, indeed, are not represented. In an effort to indicate the diversity of Israeli art today, the spaces they might have occupied were filled with works from the younger generation of Sabras—native-born Israelis[1]—who may well usher in a new period and level of accomplishment.

The wide public which this exhibition will reach should, in justice, be informed that the method of selection (which was without reference to groups or alignments), the delegation of sole authority to a juror from outside Israel, and certain of the final choices were subjects of considerable controversy when the first version of *Art Israel* opened in Jerusalem in 1964. It is apparent that no limited choice can fully represent the art of an entire nation. Nevertheless it is my hope that the exhibition and catalogue will give a valid summation of the level of quality, the intensity, and the variety of recent art in Israel, and of the themes and concerns of Israeli artists.

The diverse cultural origins of Israel, and its focal position in world affairs, tend to obscure its physical minuteness. Israel occupies a narrow wedge of land less than eight thousand square miles in area, twelve miles wide at its narrowest point, and precariously compressed between hostile neighbors and the sea; its population is about one quarter that of New York City; its history as a state began only in 1948. Yet despite the long religious tradition which forbade images, Israel today accords contemporary painting and sculpture a revered position rare among the small countries of the world. Although several of the artists in the exhibition profoundly embody Jewish culture and experience in their works, they are more citizens of one nation than they are a homogeneous cultural and religious group, and are presented as Israeli rather than Jewish artists.

The present state of art in Israel—full of potential if not yet wholly mature—is the last of several stages of development. The emergence of a regional modern art could be dated from 1906, when the Bezalel School of Arts and Crafts in Jerusalem was founded by Boris Schatz. The school combined a rather self-

[1]Those born on the territory of Israel, whether before or after formation of the state, are considered Sabras. They are named after the reddish prickly fruit that grows on the coastal plains of the country, the term referring metaphorically to their alleged characteristic of having a prickly exterior but a tender interior.

conscious emphasis on arts and crafts and a pre-impressionist realism concerned almost solely with subject matter. This initial tendency was expanded by the arrival of immigrants who knew something of European modernism, but who, like tourists, were struck by the exotic culture, the brilliant light, and the amazingly varied landscape. Thus freer realist styles, either intentionally naive or vaguely impressionist, developed. During the 1920s many of the best painters spent time in Paris, where they were influenced first by Jewish painters such as Soutine, Modigliani, Chagall, and Pascin, and by the fauves, and later by Rouault, Cézanne, Matisse, the cubists, and the figure painting of Picasso.

After the State of Israel was founded in 1948, European influences were synthesized in semi-abstract figure and landscape painting which was both emotional and decorative, and which came closer to becoming a unified national style than any work before or since, although it was plainly derivative. During the 1950s this temporary (and often superficial) unity was swept away by the tidal wave of freely brushed abstraction that was then inundating the Western art world. This now-waning "international style"—the most widespread in history—has influenced several painters represented here, although in content and spirit their art is in most cases both native and individual.

Each of these stages has left traces (not all of them fortunate) in the art of the present. Yet, as one surveys the exhibition, it is difficult to reconcile the distinct personal styles of the artists with historical and stylistic generalities. Even though any attempt to group individualistic artists is somewhat arbitrary, it will be useful, perhaps, to characterize certain of the painters in the exhibition in relation to the directions of Israel's two most influential teachers: Mordecai Ardon (Bronstein), the leading master of figurative symbolism, and Yosef Zaritsky, the leader of the New Horizons Group[2] of militant abstractionists, who, even before his trip to Paris in 1927, had begun to value relationships of form and color over subject matter. Two recurrent themes which preclude differences in style, however, can be discerned in the work of many of these artists: the tragic, an intensely felt identification with Jewish tradition and its recent trials; and the lyrical, the expression of a lighthearted love of country, which takes its form in the celebration of nature.

[2]The New Horizons Group, founded in 1948, had the following members, who exhibited together in smaller groups until 1955: the painters Pinhas Abramowitz, Mordecai Arieli, Arieh Aroch, Moshe Castel, Aharon Kahana, Avigdor Luisada, Zvi Mairovich, Avshalom Okashi, Yohanan Simon, Avigdor Stematsky, Yeheskiel Streichman, Yaacov Wexler, Marcel Yanco, and Yosef Zaritsky; and the sculptors Dov Feigin, Kosso, Moshe Sternshuss, and Ruth Zarfati-Sternshuss. After 1955 the group underwent many changes, with some artists leaving it and younger artists, such as Danziger and Shemi, becoming members.

Early in his career Ardon painted portraits and landscapes which demonstrate his worship of Rembrandt. Yet his glowing triptych of 1960, *Missa Dura,* reflects in its form and treatment his training at the Bauhaus in Weimar, his friendship with Paul Klee, and his thorough grounding in the craft of painting. Ardon's later compositions are infinitely complex montages of words, images, and signs, which give poetic expression to cabalistic religious mysteries and the joys and sorrows of Jewish experience. Even the tragedies of Hitlerism, however, are sublimated in his jewel-like palette and delicately philosophical weaving of realistic, fantastic, and abstract components.

Ardon's student Naphtali Bezem is far more specific in his theme. Like most painters of Jewish culture, Bezem is not religious in any orthodox sense: his themes have their source in his own childhood experience and return, as he says, to the history of his people. He concentrates on the theme of *aliyah*— the dramatic immigration of persecuted and rejected Jews to their historical homeland. The lion, the Torah Scroll, the Menorah, the "mute and slaughtered fish as the symbol of the Jewish people," the boat, the wheel, and the ladder commemorate in his art a drama of life unfolding from death, freedom from oppression.

Moshe Tamir, also a student of Ardon, was torn from an art of pure esthetics by the armed conflicts that followed the recognition of Israel, often referred to as the Israeli War of Independence. Only his earlier paintings in the exhibition contain recognizable symbols. Their atmosphere is fiery and apocalyptic, that of Ezekiel's vision and the Book of Revelation, of catastrophic struggles in the air. The later, abstract paintings, in their lava-like incrustation, scars, and black craters that puncture the surfaces, are more like aftermaths of natural or human struggle.

At once Jewish and broadly human in their identification, Tamir and Yigael Tumarkin employ Jewish, Christian, ancient, and modern subjects: Tamir paints *Lot's Wife* and *Satellite;* Tumarkin, *Crucifixion* and *Hiroshima.* Tumarkin works in any medium—etching, sculpture, assemblage, film, and theater, as well as painting—with astonishing facility. "It does not matter," he says, "where the artistic fact starts—with bronze, canvas, rubbish . . . what matters is to create a new reality—to create order out of disorder." No one could be less sympathetic to the "literary" qualities of Bezem than Tumarkin, yet both artists express the anguish of recent history.

In his earlier realistic and expressionistic style, Moshe Castel painted Hebrew subjects, representing folk rituals of the Sephardic and Bukharan Jewish communities. His most recent work, however, could surely be called abstract: it utilizes calligraphy, one of the few forms that were open to the Jewish artist of the past. Raised above the surface, modeled in basalt ground in oil, the hermetic script that covers his surfaces is alight with fluorescent greens, reds, and blues. It points backward to scrolls and stelae, to the Tablets of Mount Sinai.

"My art is figurative," Michael Gross quite properly states, for he paints both landscape and human beings. But these subjects are so austerely stripped of any irrelevant matter that they are often only discovered after protracted study. "While painting a man, a landscape, or any sort of figure," he says, "I am trying to arrive at the essence of a feeling within me connected with that figure or awakened by it." His stark terrains (though they often are derived from specific sites) cannot be identified. It is no surprise that Gross's approach to painting was through sculpture: his figures are lonely and monolithic. Poised at a razor-edge between recognizability and camouflage, his men and women are totally personal, but are universal in reference.

Yaacov Wexler works in the international mode of abstract expressionism and aims at "harmony and beauty." Yet he also gives expression to an essentially dramatic content. His *Triptych* seems not an impenetrable surface, but a slowly moving screen. In the sombre black skeins of paint, set off by touches of color, an atmosphere of crisis is retained.

A scholar as well as a painter, Avigdor Arikha, when he made his first drawings as a boy of sixteen, depicted Jews being herded, tortured, and killed in a German concentration camp. Later he studied with Ardon at the Bezalel School and produced an impressive series of illustrated books. His recent dark paintings flash with lightning, as does a section of sky in one of the ominous fantasies of Hieronymous Bosch. The later works are more loosely painted, but still dark, with expanding forms that break like the clouds in Baroque ceilings.

Avshalom Okashi, who is the son of a Yemenite goldsmith and rabbi and was once a shepherd in the Galilee, also employs a modern, abstract idiom. One of the first Sabra artists to develop in the new nation, Okashi, at work in his cavernous studio in the old Roman city of Acre, using immense knives he has devised to spread swaths of pigment across large canvases, seems to exemplify the meeting of a frontier and a sophisticated civilization that is typical of Israeli culture today. He returns again and again to the themes of the mystery of night and the origin of life, expressed in large areas of deep umber or black streaked with the colors of sunset or dawn, which he watches over the sea from the beaches of Acre.

The second, more lyrical strain in Israeli art is beautifully articulated in the drawings of Anna Ticho. In her earlier work she was a painstaking, almost topographical naturalist, skillfully delineating trees, plants, rocks, and the minutiae of nature; but in her most recent drawings of the great hills of Jerusalem—related to contemporary style only by the tangibility which the charcoal strokes give to empty spaces—realism ascends to ecstasy. The sure strokes give spirituality to rocks and trees even as they give form to the sweep of the wide sky above.

The lyrical tendency, as it developed along with modern style from naturalism to abstraction, was led by Yosef Zaritsky, who has been described as "the spiritual father of lyric abstraction in Israel." His sparkling, autographic watercolors of cities and landscape, mainly from the thirties, are the jewels of Israeli collections and are among the finest watercolors of the twentieth century. His large abstract oils of the fifties and sixties are at home among paintings from many countries; but, because Zaritsky is not well enough known in America, it should be emphasized that their manner is as original and individual as, let us say, Hans Hofmann's. The shifting lozenges of color, separated and heightened by white and united by relaxed movements of a loaded brush, have a characteristic and unique asymmetrical structure. Though abstract, these large compositions, often almost square, remain naturalistic and lyrical in effect.

Yeheskiel Streichman is also one of the leading abstract artists of Israel. He considers himself a Zionist painter. Like many other Israeli artists, he fought and was wounded in the War of Independence. Yet he almost bitterly rejects the use of Jewish "literary, religious, and philosophical symbols" as "merely a way of exploiting sentiment." In every sense an "abstract impressionist" he sees his precursors as Tiepolo, Fragonard, and Monet. In the web of delicately toned and carefully organized strokes that make up Streichman's large compositions, one sees the pinks and yellows of spring, the tans and reds of the Negev desert, and in such a canvas as *After Poussin,* bacchanalian celebration of life within nature.

Landscape painting was also the starting point of Yehiel Krize, who was a student of Zaritsky and whose work is now radically abstract. "There is not a single spot in Israel that I did not see and paint," he recalls. His most recent oils, in which almost uniform surfaces are woven with strokes of extreme sensitivity, again reflect the lyrical strain.

Zvi Mairovich, one of the founders of the New Horizons Group, also began with nature, but has developed a more rugged style than that of Streichman or Krize. Nonfigurative at first glance, his solidly built compositions are landscapes, however generalized, and are so titled. Their bold forms evoke varied imagery, from the rocky formations and red earth of the Negev to trees, flowers, and water seen in sun and shade.

The skillful and tense watercolors and oils of Avigdor Stematsky resemble landscapes, for they are created, as he says, from "angles . . . slope . . . the issue of the earth . . . light and shadow." One finds in them a concentration of both dramatic and lyrical feeling. Some are pale and open in form; others are sombre, suggesting the ochre masonry walls of Jerusalem. The splashed reds and blue-blacks of the watercolors call to mind blood and tears as well as rain.

Paris has been Israel's closest link with the international art world, and an important group of artists divide their time between Israel and France. In part because she lived in Paris between 1950 and 1962, Léa Nikel was one of the first Israeli painters to turn from realism to abstraction, though she never broke her connection with Israel or Israeli artists, who regard her work highly. She emphasizes the act of painting itself as well as the brilliance of landscape and light, in canvases which are small in size but bold and varied in color and attack. Despite their size, her oils have more affinity with New York action painting than does the work of any of the artists mentioned above.

Among the Israeli painters who have lived in Paris is Fima. Few countries in the world have concentrated men from such diverse backgrounds in so small an area as has Israel. The career of Fima offers a case in point. Born in China of Russian parents, versed as a young man in Chinese and Japanese calligraphy and painting, he arrived in Israel in 1949. Although quite at home in the School of Paris, he retains a touch of the Orient in his paintings. They recall the mountain and water painting of China and the decorative scrolls of Japan.

David Lan-Bar believes in "painting that is called 'Jewish,' even if it belongs to the Paris School," and is convinced that the future of art lies in abstraction. He works in a painterly, tightly-packed, and knowledgeable style. In the many layers of thoughtful strokes that make up his dense surfaces, a history can be seen: the emotional tone of expressionism, the structure of classical cubism; even the form of the human figure leaves its trace, though the artist has turned away from it.

Although Yaacov Agam, a Sabra and the son of a rabbi, is influenced by Hebraic thinking and has executed important commissions for the Israeli government, his art has nothing—visually at least—to do with Jewish tradition. It is almost the only "hard-edge" abstraction in Israeli art. Agam can be encountered by chance in nearly any Western city, but he does most of his work in his Paris workshop, where machine tools, wood, aluminum, and paint in cans replace easels, tubes, and palettes. Now holding a secure position in international art circles, Agam was a pioneer both in "kinetic" art manipulated by the spectator, which uses "the dimension of time," and in "optical" composition, in which flat colors and simple shapes appear, blend, and disappear as the spectator changes position.

At one time sculpture in the round was forbidden to Jews by rabbinical law. Originally because of this, and later because of the difficulties of solving technical problems in periods of disruption, sculpture developed later than painting in Israel. Nevertheless it is possible that public sculpture will become one of the most original achievements of the new nation. In sharp contrast with much American sculpture, which is geared to a dealer-collector market, sculpture in Israel is moving toward monumentality and interaction with the variety of the land and the life of the people. Inspired in part by Itzhak Danziger, an important member of the New Horizons Group and a leader of young artists whose influence is comparable to Zaritsky's, the reclamation of the Negev Desert and other large public projects are giving birth to an indigenous concept of form and space. Like the severe but sometimes beautiful ferro-concrete water towers that dot the Israeli landscape, the new conceptions—most of them still in the minds of their creators, or existing only in sketches—merge sculpture with architecture and nature, utility with pure or symbolic form.

Danziger's public monuments in steel and stone gave early promise of the new Israeli sculpture. His recently finished work *"The Lord is My Shepherd"* (*Negev Sheep*), which was completed and destroyed several times during the past thirteen years, symbolizes his desire to conform with the great masses, forces, and expanses of the desert rather than futilely to strive to dominate them, for "the desert does not tolerate any false gestures." A potent and ancient symbol, the sheep connotes in this work the need for water, shelter from the blistering sun, food and clothing, even the precarious existence of the nation.

Shamai Haber, though he lives in Paris, thinks entirely in Mediterranean terms and prefers to work in granite—"the heaviest material, the most dynamic, the hardest." His works in this exhibition are small, for those that interest him most (such as his monument for the building designed by Philip Johnson for the atomic reactor at Rehovot) are far too large and heavy to travel. He has evolved an original sculptural form—massive stone elements in delicate equilibrium—but looks forward to creating sculptured desert towns rather than "little sculptures on pedestals."

Kosso Eloul also uses stone more than any other medium and has been a leader in the current international "symposiums" of sculpture, in which artists from many countries work individually at a single site to create the monumental works which recent architectural thinking demands, but which sculptors have as yet rarely provided. But Kosso's art is more personal than Danziger's or Haber's. Like the painter Michael Gross, Kosso strives for essences. He seeks to "make visible a *symbol* . . . to make a special, personal gesture, an offering, a moment of meditation, a sacrifice." By making sharp cuts in the primary form of his "objects"—columns, altars, gates, and menhirs—he energizes these static and ancient symbols with the dynamic gestures of the present.

As in the United States and Europe, in Israel sculptors salvage scrap metal as a major material. But as one passes the rusting hulks of abandoned military vehicles that line the road between Tel Aviv and Jerusalem, it becomes evident that for Israelis such material recalls combat and victory. The war monuments of Danziger and Tumarkin retain this reference. In the studio of Yehiel Shemi at Kibbutz Cabri, however, old metal plates, rails, sheets, and bars are transformed into compositions that, though masculine and powerful, can rise with the freedom of flame or water, or with the delicacy of flowers. "A sculpture bursting forth into space," he says, "is comparable to an organic creation of nature. It . . . develops as does a plant, a tree, or a human being." It is Shemi's ability to mold stubborn material with apparent ease, to find inspired meetings of strength and fluidity, that in part constitutes his importance as a sculptor.

As a sampling of the newest talent in Israeli art, three representatives of the impatient young generation of Sabras round out the selection. Ezra Orion, a tractor driver at Kibbutz Beit Alpha, has created his two graceful and powerful works of sculpture in spare time and on the one day a week he is able to leave his labor. Raffi Lavie has originated a sophisticated "infantilistic" but sensitively ordered style that is courageous and free of European influence. Aïka, on the other hand, worked in both Paris and Israel before his recent tragic death, and was thus in close contact with international trends. He combined painting and assemblage, using the latter quite recently as the basis of interesting sculpture in bronze.

During the preparation of this exhibition I was asked several times if some quality characteristically Israeli, common to all the work I had seen, could be discerned. The question is more wishful, perhaps, than it should be: homogeneity in the art of a group, region, or nation can be a vice as well as a virtue. Nevertheless, avoiding specious assertions of unity, one other mediating element should be pointed out in addition to the two tendencies— lyrical and dramatic—discussed above. Let us call it *intensity*. The intensity of the human compassion, pride, intellect, and creativity that gave form to the State of Israel itself is still the prime source of energy that activates Israeli art and gives it a distinctive aura, whatever the style. The very pressure of the concentrated life is a motive force which, I believe, will result in an even higher level of achievement in the future.

WILLIAM C. SEITZ

Yaacov Agam

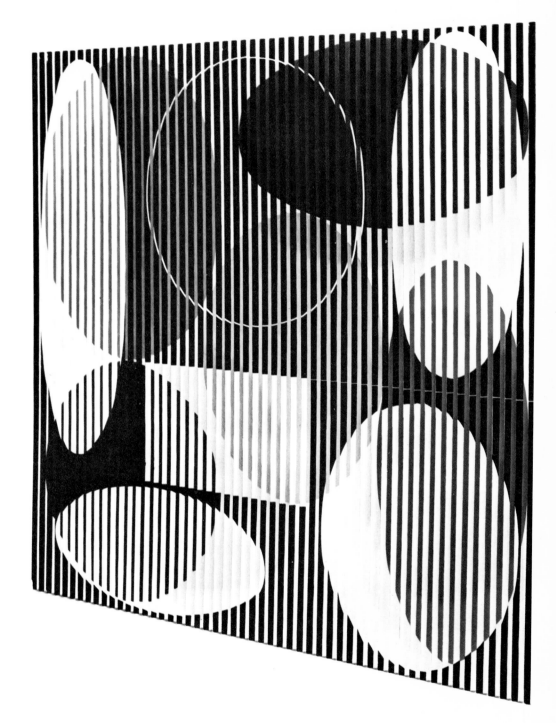

LEFT: Yaacov Agam: *Four Themes-Counterpoint.* 1959. Oil on wood. Galerie Israel Ltd.

BELOW: Yaacov Agam: *Diptyque Painting.* 1962–63. Oil on wood. Collection the artist, courtesy of Marlborough-Gerson Gallery.

Statement by the Artist

My endeavor has been to create a kind of painting existing not only in space but in the time in which it develops and evolves and thus producing a foreseeable infinity of plastic situations flowing out of one another, whose successive apparitions and disappearances provide ever-renewed revelations.

The introduction of the dimension of time, of duration, and of continuity into the pictorial experience enables us to penetrate more deeply into the essence of a work, which, in spite of, or perhaps because of, its outer transformations, all the more effectively preserves its organic unity and its ineffaceable inner identity.

Whereas traditional painting enabled the artist only to execute the portrait of a person in a given situation and in a precise state of mind, and whereas contemporary painting can only suggest a definite plastic situation and state of mind, the "portrait" that I propose to make of a pictorial reality resembles a living person who, whatever be his movements, his state of mind, and his appearance, remains himself with his own identity, and who in his multiple contacts with the outer world assumes, according to the situation, a different form resulting from all the states that are virtually a part of him. My intention has been to introduce into each work a life of its own, so that the work should acquire an autonomous existence, parallel to that of the viewer....

From *Yaakov Agam*, Neuchatel: Editions du Griffon, 1962.

3

4

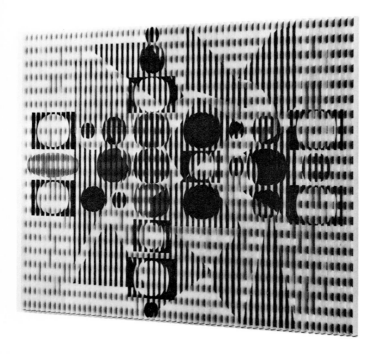

5

6

Aïka

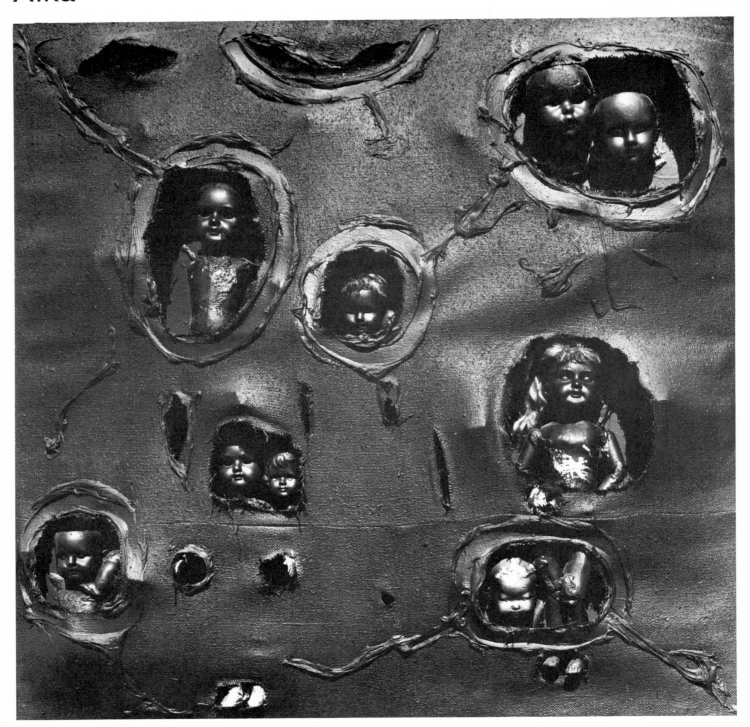

Aïka: *Dolls I*. 1964. Plastic materials with dolls. Mrs. Yardena Brown.

21

Statement by the Artist

Parts of dolls—disjointed hands and legs, heads without eyes, ears and hair—it seems at first glance that the right place for this rubbish should be the garbage can or some flea market. Yesterday little girls played with them in their rooms and prams and today I play the game.

Such was the first doll I found—I took it from a garbage can that first year I was in Paris in 1959. It was in the coal shop where I lived and worked for about a year that I did my first black picture with pieces of dolls and other rubbish.

I breathed into these objects my life's breath, conferring on them eternity.

In my subconscious they certainly serve a specific purpose, at this moment secondary.

My way of working is spontaneous, quick; I work on a number of canvases simultaneously. It is the materials I use that call for such a way of working and indeed determine the results.

It may happen that tomorrow other objects will draw my attention, but the unending search will always give the specific character to my works. I belong to the second half of the twentieth century, and it is only logical that I work in this way and no other.

To live in one's own time should be the aim of every artist—the means may vary, but never the goal.

Tel Aviv, 1964

LEFT: Aïka: *White and Black Relief.* 1964. Plastic materials. Mrs. Yardena Brown.

ABOVE: Aïka: *Relief Composition.* 1963. Plastic materials. Mrs. Yardena Brown.

Mordecai Ardon

Mordecai Ardon: *Missa Dura*. 1958–60. Oil.
By courtesy of the Trustees of the Tate Gallery.

Statement by the Artist

. . . something disturbing happened on my palette: something odd sneaked into the cadmiums, ultramarines, and viridians—it was Jerusalem, ascetic, with a sack over her head.

How does Jerusalem come to be amongst the light cadmiums? How can one scrape her off the palette? At times, perhaps, she can be submerged beneath the ivory black. But in vain—for on the morrow she reappears among the cadmiums.

That's the problem! For thousands of years, Jerusalem has been protesting against Athens—Athens the radiant, the Apollonian . . . Athens the Dionysian. How I admire Athens! How godlike and lightly does a Matisse wander to and fro there: the sweet waters of the Mediterranean sweeten his canvases—the morning fragrances waft over them.

At such moments Jerusalem creeps away, far beneath the black. But no sooner has Matisse passed—than she reveals herself again amongst the cadmiums, the ultramarines, and the viridians.

There's no getting away from it! This strange Jerusalem always has some command to give: "Thou shalt! . . ." "Thou shalt not! . . ."—like a black woodpecker Jerusalem pecks at you—thou . . . thou . . . thou—thou and the orphan—thou and the widow—thou and the distressed—thou and the oppressed. . . .

From a letter of the artist to W. Sandberg, former Director of the Amsterdam Municipal Museums, now Adviser to the Israel Museum, Jerusalem.   Jerusalem, 1960.

FAR LEFT: Mordecai Ardon: *Timepecker.* 1963. Oil and tempera. Collection the artist.

LEFT: Mordecai Ardon: *The Way to Jerusalem.* 1962. Oil. Bezalel National Museum, gift of Mrs. Katharine Sonneborn Falk. (New York showing only.)

Avigdor Arikha

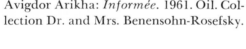

Statement by the Artist

What does the painter do? He lets a surface accomplish its own organization through the operation of the hand. Out of this may come the revelation of a quality up till now invisible.

Traces of a passage through time, set down in a state of emergency.

Seen from outside, a totality signalled at the level of sensation.

1964

Avigdor Arikha: *Informée.* 1961. Oil. Collection Dr. and Mrs. Benensohn-Rosefsky.

RIGHT: Avigdor Arikha: *Noirs Précipités.* 1963. Oil. Collection the artist.

LEFT: Avigdor Arikha: *Incandescences.* 1959. Oil. Collection the artist.

Naphtali Bezem

Naphtali Bezem: *The Common Grave*. 1962. Oil. Collection the artist.

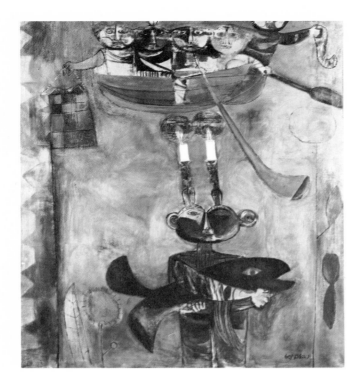

Naphtali Bezem: *Coming Back*. 1960. Oil. Collection the artist.

Naphtali Bezem: *Rising Figure*. 1963. Oil. Collection the artist.

Statement by the Artist

Throughout my work, motifs such as mute and slaughtered fish as the symbol of the Jewish people, the weeping lion of Judah as the surviving mourner, Jacob's ladder reaching to heaven, candlesticks . . . —together with all kinds of imaginary objects—give me great freedom and stimulation in composition. The people in the pictures are always immigrants like myself or like my parents would have been if they had come to Israel—so they often have wings. . . . They come in boats which sail the skies and land in the sacred desert. All this gives my paintings a . . . surrealistic touch mingled with a little sad humor.

I can say very little about my philosophy of painting. I feel that painting must mean something. . . . Thus, in my own work, I find it impossible to separate the symbolic content from the means of expressing it; only if both complement each other does the picture seem good to me. Of course, this is nothing new, for good painting has always been so.

Naturally, I find my subjects in my background, although I am not religious. I reach down into my childhood—sometimes to the very depths of my mother's womb—and on my return voyage I do not stop there, but continue back into the history of my people who, in my paintings, come to life.

By nature, I am an experimenter, so techniques interest me enormously. I mix media such as oil, casein, plastic, etc. My constant preoccupation with materials and the clear knowledge that I am dealing with "matter" and not with "spirit" keeps me from becoming literary. Sometimes the subject emerges from the matter during the painting and I change [a painting] several times before I am satisfied that spirit and matter are indivisible.

Tel Aviv, 1963

Moshe Castel

Moshe Castel: *Manuscrit de Neguev*. 1964. Pulverized basalt mixed in oil. Galerie Karl Flinker.

LEFT: Moshe Castel: *Poésie de Canaan I*. 1963.
Pulverized basalt mixed in oil.
The Museum of Modern Art,
gift of Mr. and Mrs. David Kluger.

Statement on the Artist

To me, one of the characteristics of contemporary Israeli art is its emphasis on international themes and techniques. Upon viewing exhibits by some of the young country's most talented painters, I am often left with the feeling that they demonstrate little that is authentically Israeli, Hebrew, or even Jewish; the canvases could as easily have been produced by French, Italian, or American abstractionists. This observation is not meant as a value judgment. One can understand the determination of Israelis to maintain their intellectual connections with the West, to demonstrate their liberation, culturally at least, from the parochialism of the Levant.

Moshe Castel is an important exception to this subconscious trend in Israeli painting. He is, to be sure, an artist of international stature, acclaimed by critics in Europe and America as a master craftsman and a poetic imagist. His uniqueness, however, does not lie merely in his original techniques, in his daring and imaginative use of coruscating hues, his ingenious utilization of melted basalt for texture. I believe that his distinctiveness is to be found, rather, in his subject matter. Castel's themes spring from the innocent anthropomorphism of the Bible, the awakened dream-legends of the medieval Cabala, the charming and graceful folk rituals of Palestine's veteran Sephardic and Bukharan Jewish communities. The motifs are integral to the country. But they are also the personal inheritance of Castel's family. The Castels came to Palestine originally as refugees from medieval Spain and have lived in the Holy Land for five centuries, producing in each

generation rabbis, cabalists, faith heal-
ers, and musicians. Their memories and
traditions, superbly conceived and recon-
structed, form the animating vision of all
Castel's painting. Indeed, more than any
artist of his time, Castel is the palimpsest
of Jewish Israel.

Significantly, it is this "Hebrew" quality
which audiences have found to be the
most captivating aspect of Castel's work.
I am convinced that this public response
represents more than fascination with the
exotic. Indeed, the words "authentic,"
"integral," "deep-rooted," are the adjec-
tives most frequently invoked in the de-
scriptions of Castel's painting. This
should hardly be surprising. The most
enduring art, whether in literature, music, or painting, has always faithfully re-
flected the soul of the artist and his people. Nothing has ever been more banal
than a trackless search for an "international" style. On the contrary, fidelity to
what is best—the most characteristic, the
most poignantly faithful, the most mean-
ingful—in an artist's own folk milieu has
almost invariably struck the most respon-
sive chords on both local and foreign soil.
Nothing is more universal than the particular—the particular faithfully conceived, beautifully crafted, richly and he-
roically projected. By these criteria,
Moshe Castel is an artist of universal dimensions.

Note on the artist by Abram Leon Sachar, Presi-
dent of Brandeis University, Waltham, Massachusetts, in the exhibition catalog *Castel*, LeFebre
Gallery, New York, 1964.

Moshe Castel: *Poésie de Canaan*. 1964. Pulverized basalt mixed in
oil. Collection of the Knesset, gift of Mr. and Mrs. David Kluger.
Courtesy of Lefebre Gallery. (New York showing only.)

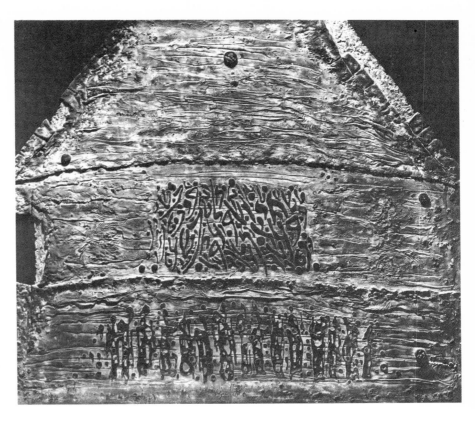

Moshe Castel: *Untitled*. 1964. Pulverized basalt mixed in oil. Lefebre Gallery.
(Showings outside New York only.)

Itzhak Danziger

Itzhak Danziger: *"The Lord is my Shepherd"* (*Negev Sheep*). 1964. Bronze. The Joseph H. Hirshhorn Collection.

RIGHT: Itzhak Danziger: *Sculpture*. 1959. Welded iron. Galerie Israel Ltd.

33

Statement by the Artist

A sculpture should not be an "exhibition piece" for a museum, as it still is in Europe—a result of an epigonic, highly refined tradition which has existed for hundreds of years in art.

It should be active and its function multiple—it should unify or divide space, form a part of the landscape, indicate direction. . . . It should be alive in an ambiance—in perpetual rapport with its given surroundings. The inspiration of a sculpture should come from a sense of rootedness in the land, the landscape, and the nation—from thorough knowledge of the topography, the geography, and national values of the land and its people.

Sheep are one of the basic images of the desert. I tried to concretize in this sculpture ["The Lord is My Shepherd" (Negev Sheep)] *the whole landscape and significance of the Negev. As a matter of fact, the desert is without competition: it is immense. In order to give expression to it, one has to be modest and anonymous. The desert does not tolerate any false gestures. It destroys one who does not know how to adapt himself to its exigencies. The other basic element of the desert is water. Its vital value has not changed for 4,000 years. Technical progress in storing it has been insignificant in comparison with its intrinsic value. I am also occupied with the problem of the well in the conception of the Negev's sculptural expression. It is logical that a sculpture is not an isolated esthetic item. It is part of a landscape, of a city, of a garden—which are in themselves sculptured spaces and planned sculptures. It is, perhaps, an attempt to give form to a new sociology and ideology of a better life—as the cathedral was in the past.*

Tel Aviv, 1964

Fima

Fima: *Village in the Mountains*. 1962. Oil. Collection the artist, courtesy of Galerie Jacques Massol.

LEFT: Fima: *Mountain Landscape*. 1963. Oil. Collection the artist, courtesy of Galerie Jacques Massol.

Statement by the Artist

Nature provides the inspiration for a painter's work. It is a starting point; no theme has ever added anything to the quality of painting. Good art is always abstract and perennially young, whether it is a portrait or a square; good art is also full of deep secrets of inner experience, not secrets of technique.

In my own art I strive to give life to the square, or rather, the picture, to solve it, to open up broad spaces, so that the elements should be free to transcend it and to continue their life outside the canvas. I strive to build the surface rightly, to find the right tone, the pristine freshness of the picture, whose surface should radiate light and air.

My painting is an art of transposition, suggestive, built on memories and associations, and it happens that an abyss becomes sky, while the movement of a fish or the flight of a bird becomes the choreography of a dance and some color alliances become musical sounds. The surface sometimes recalls Chinese porcelain, in which colors and elements are drowned, while transparent elements rise to the fore. As I lived in China during my first thirty-two years, the fact cannot be denied that my work shows the influence and partly the attitude of the Far East—a predominantly lyrical attitude. Here and there appear structures based on the rhythms of Chinese calligraphy, both in the straight delineating sense of the term, and the deeper sense. . . . I work with both a European and a Far Eastern conception of painting; my aim is to create a link between the Far East and Europe through vision. I do not strive to achieve a renewal of the art of painting, as, in my opinion, painting is eternally nonrenewable; only creative vision is renewed.

Paris, 1964

Michael Gross

Michael Gross: *Small Figure on Blue*. 1964. Casein on composition board. Collection the artist.

I love art in which feelings and instincts reach spiritual sublimation—true sublimation, wherein distillation and extraction strengthen more and more the human motive, which is really the source and condition of every true art of any kind and style—art from which the very cord of life is woven.

My art is figurative. The inner powers speak through the images of the figures causing them. While painting a man, a landscape, or any sort of figure, I am trying to arrive at the essence of a feeling within me connected with that figure or awakened by it.

The painted figure strives to refine these emotional aspects, by its tense means of color and form, to a degree of symbolism.

I love the naked light of our landscape— luminous plains, clear and distinct, the far like the near in form and color—pulsating in tangible, spiritual tension—the Kinereth.

The sun in its intensity powerfully permeates and saturates the colors—a fusion of strength and delicacy. Landscape is truly the school of painting.

But more and more I would like to say something about man—wherever one moves he touches you; so much beauty, more pain, sorrow, and loneliness.

I believe through loyalty to and deep probing into the truths of life we shall build within generations our own art; it will come naturally with the growth and formation of our life.

The universal value of art depends solely on the emotional and spiritual values of art, independent of the external phrasing.

True style is that emerging from inner qualities seeking expression.

1964

LEFT: Michael Gross: *Figure in Ochre*. 1963. Oil. Collection the artist.

Michael Gross: *Woman in Black*. 1963. Oil. Collection the artist.

Michael Gross: *Plain in Blazing Sun*. 1964. Oil on paper mounted on plywood.
Collection Mr. and Mrs. Gidon Schocken.

Michael Gross: *Slain Soldier in the Field*. 1964. Oil. Collection the artist.

Shamai Haber

Shamai Haber: *Small Monument*. 1962. Brittany granite. Collection the artist.

Statement by the Artist

I have always sought the monumental in my sculpture. From the beginning of this century sculpture has been evolving from more or less appealing objects—torsos, busts, etc., executed in fine materials—to abstract shapes. I soon realized that putting abstract shapes on conventional bases has been outlived and is not fitting in our "plastic civilization." I did away with bases and pedestals and started creating from the soil itself. The truth is that an object that is not essential, that does not represent anything and is a creation of plastic fantasy alone, does not need a pretext (a pedestal of 1.8 m. for a 20 cm. high object!).

In clearing the soil with bulldozers in the Negev desert and then planting there 100 tons of granite, I suddenly became aware of the fact that my sculpture in itself is as important as the angle created between it and the soil, or the distance between the sculpture and the nearest building, etc.

When I returned to Paris after having finished this monument in Israel, I felt I had done enough of sculpture of dimensions limited by gallery and exhibition conditions. I had always been independent, refusing to work for an art dealer or to be limited in any way. After long walks from the Coupole to the Dome and to the Select, I went to my studio and built in a void-shape that can be augmented in different ways and a thousand times (as can all my sculpture). I realized that I had chanced to create a vital space that can help solve the habitation problem in the desert. . . . I had achieved freshness as well as protection from light. I invited town planners to see my sculpture; they were impressed with the idea and offered their collaboration. From that moment I was saved. I began creating this utopian space. I created a desert, and in that desert I built a town. To create a city in the desert—this is my GOAL! I received technical advice and professional support. I contacted sociologists who had worked in the Middle East. And now, I am there in a desert of my own imagination—in this city of fantasy that I hope will one day be built. And, for all my friends—I reserve an apartment there.

Shamai Haber: *Untitled.* 1960–61. Brittany granite. Collection Mr. and Mrs. Albert A. List.

Paris, 1964

Kosso

43

Kosso: *Statement*. 1962. Bronze. Collection the artist.

LEFT: Kosso: *Doubleself*. 1962. Travertine stone. Collection Lee A. Kolker. (New York showing only.)

Statement by the Artist

A statement on my sculpture?—you are asking me to attempt to look instantaneously at both sides of the coin and catch the end result and the initial impulse, the being-doing at the very same instant by the very same man. You demand simultaneous inward and outward awareness, depth-involvement and far away detachment, or we shall miss all connections, or become fragmentary—can I do it?

What is sculpture for me?—a thought, a principle one stands by, made visible. Never a description nor an illustration. If I were religious, I'd say the visualizing and the making of the gods of our times and the reaching for the new gods of the times yet to come.

I suppose it's the same urge which forced prehistoric man—who had hunted and got his meat, had his woman, and was not hungry any more—to take tools in his hands and instead of sensibly sleeping on the hot sands, to go and carve a form, a shape, which became an affirmation of his existence on this earth—his God—his touch with the unknown and his anchor on life—the life of his times.

Thus:

The art of sculpture is a human technique to reach and make visible a symbol. To achieve a symbol to which I would feel compelled—by its own strength; to make a special, personal gesture, an offering, a moment of meditation, a sacrifice; to be personally, deeply involved, regenerated by its energy, excited by its vision; to be proud of being able to see it and experience it—the doubling of the integrity involved—that is sculpture for me. The visual experience is total. It is so "whole," so instantaneous, so direct and immediate, transmitted to all levels of the being, the receiver, from the sensuous-physical to the philosophical-principle strata.

This visual encounter-experience cannot even accept the time lag needed to read these words. Yet, if we accept this limitation as a characteristic trait of our medium—and employ it as such—it becomes great strength—the strength of the visual-hypnotic-regenerating power of sculpture.

Tel Aviv, 1964

Kosso: *Basic*. 1963. Jerusalem stone. Collection Lee A. Kolker.

Kosso: *Altar*. 1964. Jerusalem stone. Collection the artist.

Yehiel Krize

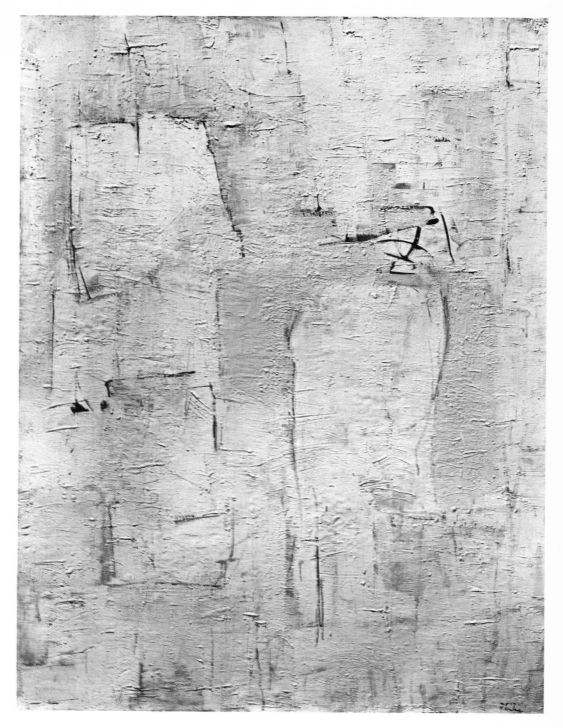

Yehiel Krize: *Painting*. 1961. Oil. Collection the artist.

Statement by the Artist

I think I never have been "figurative."
As far as I remember I also painted "flat."
This might be because I started out while
very young as a weaver. Weaving is based
on crossing rhythms. Later I was attracted
to the sea—its flatness and its rhythms.
Then during the years I lived in orange
groves, I acquired a vision of a flat, clear,
monochrome universe.

I painted also a whole year with Yosef
Zaritsky. From the very beginning this
probably solved problems of principle. I
am a landscape painter. From my child-
hood I was exposed a great deal to nature.
There is not a single spot in Israel that I
did not see and paint, whether it be Ein-
Karem, the Carmel, the Dead Sea, or the
Mediterranean.

There are perhaps very prosaic reasons
for my not having become a still-life
painter: I never painted fruits, flowers,
objects . . . the apartment we lived in was
too small; there was no place for an easel.

I painted in gouache for years, out of
doors, sitting right on the ground.

I hope the evolution I underwent is sen-
sitive. With time I spanned the space,
made my painting more silent and essen-
tial in its expression.

Tel Aviv, 1964

Yehiel Krize: *Composition*. 1964. Gouache on paper. Collection the artist.

49

Yehiel Krize: *Composition*. 1964. Gouache on paper. Collection the artist.

David Lan-Bar

51

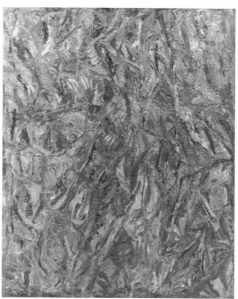

David Lan-Bar: *Composition 859*.
1963. Oil. Collection the artist.

Statement by the Artist

I believe in complex painting—in terms of subject and color. I also believe in a painting that is called "Jewish," even if it belongs to the Paris School.

I believe in abstract art—that is to say, freedom from the direct, daily subject that is recognizable to the eye at first glance.

A painting's influence should come from the painting's "inner life." In short, a painting should be majestic. In any case, it should not be an expression of the exterior environment.

Color, composition, line, and movement are elements of a pictorial language and not of any other. Only through them is it possible to understand and to decipher a picture. The future of painting is that of liberated and abstract art.

Paris, 1964

ABOVE: David Lan-Bar: *Composition 726*. 1960. Oil. Collection the artist.

LEFT: David Lan-Bar: *Composition 854*. 1962. Oil. Collection the artist.

Raffi Lavie

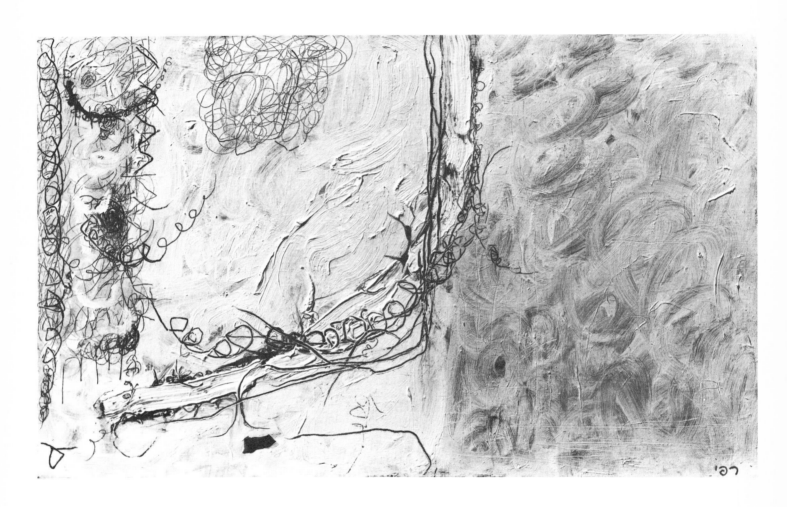

Raffi Lavie: *Painting 95*. 1963. Oil, pencil, and charcoal. Rina Gallery.

53

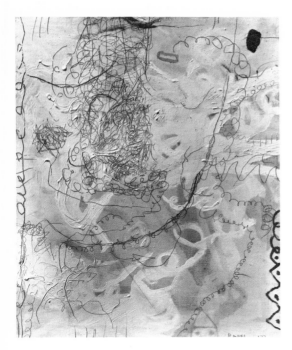

Raffi Lavie: *Painting 98.* 1963. Oil, pencil, and charcoal. Rina Gallery.

Statement by the Artist

To tell the truth, *I do not like painting. I paint because I cannot do otherwise. It is for me like eating, sleeping—a natural function.*

I paint spontaneously, directly. Movement plays an important role; in fact, I paint with my whole body, although I do not subscribe to the "action painting" school, which often seems to me to be superficial.

I love children's painting. A child forgets himself and therefore paints independently and uninhibitedly — straightforwardly and directly.

Tel Aviv, 1964

Raffi Lavie: *Painting 100.* 1963. Oil and pencil. Rina Gallery.

Zvi Mairovich

ABOVE: Zvi Mairovich: *Dead Sea Landscape.*
1963. Oil. Collection the artist.

RIGHT: Zvi Mairovich: *Mitzpe-Ramon Landscape.* 1964. Oil. Collection the artist.

Zvi Mairovich: *Mitzpe-Ramon Landscape.* 1964. Oil. Collection the artist.

Statement by the Artist

I paint nature. To me it is the desire to return to the primary awareness of sight. Then comes the whirlpool. Also the conciseness, and something tangible. The cruelty of limitation results from the mute forcefulness of nature. Something immutable takes possession of you. The Mitzpe-Ramon landscape. A strip of eternal red-violet land, unattainable, overwhelms you again and again. I cannot think of anything more powerful or more novel. And there I find myself thrust back at my starting point.

And the precious moment is something like a miracle, the appearance of the reciprocation between the painter and the vision. The artistic fact has a nature of its own, and the nature of an artistic fact does not change. The interpretation plays a secondary role only. Interpretations are interesting only if they come from the same source as that of art itself. When I say that I paint nature, I refer to this kind of anxiety. I feel it when the canvas begins to break away from the vision of nature and attacks me with its own phenomenon, just as nature attacks me from another angle. I do not wish to exaggerate, but something fatal happens then. Something alive is being created from the living. The canvas has then a life of its own. And I long for a clear rhythm that has something of the hidden.

1964

Léa Nikel

Léa Nikel: *Composition*. 1963. Oil. Collection the artist.

Léa Nikel: *Composition.* 1963.
Oil. Collection the artist.

Léa Nikel: *Composition 9.*
1960. Oil. Collection
Mr. and Mrs. Israel Zafrir.

Statement on the Artist

. . . Braque once declared that he wanted to create "an art before which one would stand without thinking anything." This sentence could serve as a motto for Nikel's work.

Until Israel was established in 1948 the local painters, who drew so much from the tradition of the Jewish painters in Eastern and Western Europe, emphasized line and drawing rather than color.

Léa Nikel, who spent about fifteen years in Paris, represents the minor revolution introduced into Israeli painting by a number of younger artists who strove to liberate color from the domination of line. Her paintings are "festivals of color." Here there is nothing which is not purely dramatic; neither atmosphere nor symbols nor even the expression of a mood.

Form defined through line or dot has vanished from these canvases. Here and there whorls of paint which have come straight from the tube seem to define linearly a colored spot or area; but essentially speaking, for Nikel a line is only "the direction of the color-form."

Her range of colors is rich and sometimes sharp in its unsophisticated contrasts. There is a definite tendency to employ explicit colors at the expense of gradations and tones. . . . Her work gives the impression of unforced spontaneity, of arbitrary pleasure, which often challenges the eye of the beholder in these canvases so soaked in the joy of living and the love of color.

Note on the artist by Nathan Zach in the catalog of the XXXII Biennale, Venice, 1964.

Avshalom Okashi

59

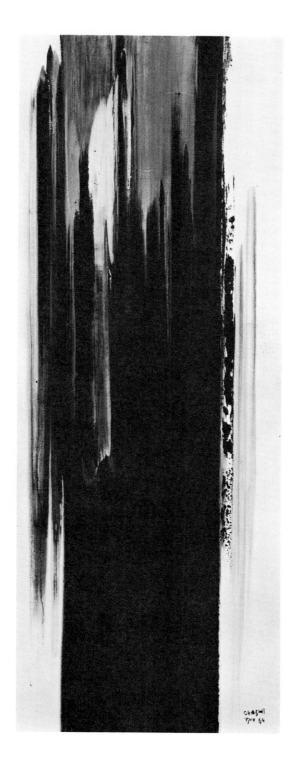

Statement by the Artist

The basic principle of the pictorial impact lies in the fact of the liberation of masses of light and shadow that succeed in pursuing each other. No detail, but rather the painting as a whole, determines the theme.

It is only through the sum total of the parts that the secret of the synthesis of light, form, and color can be realized. It is clear that what happens here is not a material, corporeal fact—just as the human being is not made up only of flesh and bones.

All artistic observation is directly connected with the scope of the painting.

It happens, therefore, that the world takes shape in the eye according to specific forms, and in every new materialization there is revealed a new aspect of the message of the world.

One cannot avoid the fact that this new aspect runs historically parallel to the national human characteristic and that the most important qualities are embodied in national values. The vision goes beyond these values and is realized within the boundaries of art.

National differences in the artistic vision are not a matter of taste alone; they comprise the principles of the entire concept of the whole universe of a nation.

Acre, 1964

LEFT: Avshalom Okashi: *The Prayer.* 1964. Polyvinyl acetate. Galerie Israel Ltd.

FAR LEFT: Avshalom Okashi: *Untitled No. 2.* 1964. Oil and basalt. Betty Parsons Gallery.

Ezra Orion

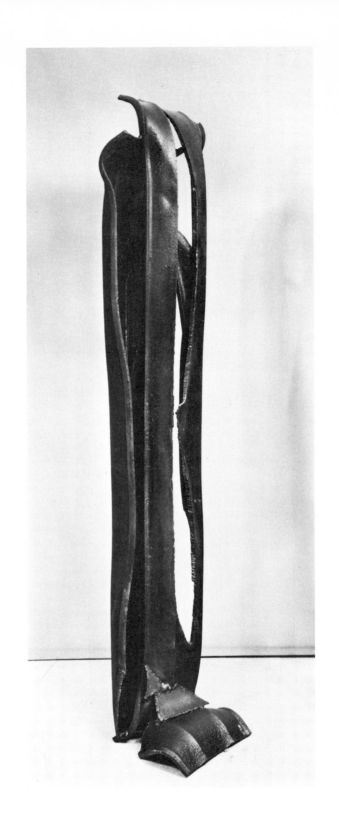

61

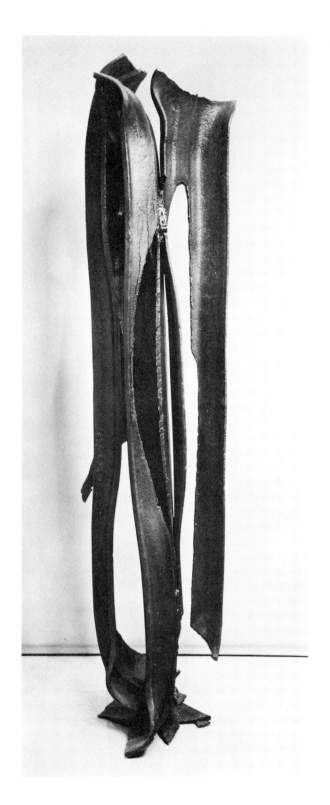

Statement by the Artist

  The expression of iron is somehow bitter. Iron gives me a feeling of harshness and strength, which is felt even in the soft points of the sculpture.

Kibbutz Beit Alpha, 1964

FAR LEFT: Ezra Orion: *High Night I*. 1963. Welded iron. Collection the artist.

LEFT: Ezra Orion: *High Night II*. 1963. Welded iron. Collection the artist.

Yehiel Shemi

Yehiel Shemi: *Standing I*. 1963.
Welded iron. Collection the artist.

Statement by the Artist

A sculpture bursting forth into space is comparable to an organic creation of nature. It is built step by step and develops as does a plant, a tree, or a human being.

Iron construction distinguishes itself by its power and allows me to make concrete my conception in sculpture. In that way, a new and particular tension is created between the different real and imagined bodies.

In iron works, be they chiseled or hammered, I see poetry and a new esthetic sensation which suits our times.

From the catalog of the exhibition *Yehiel Shemi,* Bezalel National Museum, Jerusalem, 1957.

Yehiel Shemi: *Sculpture.* 1963. Welded iron. Collection the artist.

Yehiel Shemi: *Sculpture.* 1963. Welded iron. Collection the artist.

Avigdor Stematsky

Statement by the Artist

My painting is not realistic, though its roots are in nature and in reality. I am sensitive to angles and to slope, to the issue of the earth, to light and shadow. These are the elements of which my painting is created. Abstraction is for me a liberation as well as a duty to express the concentration and intensification of art and life.

Critics try to limit painting to the narrow confines of one trend or another. The painting itself is the only law for the painter.

The painter's work is one of ant-like tedium, and at the same time, it is invested with the force of fresh torrential streams, which the painter often beholds upon breaking through stone walls.

Tel Aviv, 1964

LEFT: Avigdor Stematsky: *Painting.* 1962. Oil. Collection the artist.

BELOW: Avigdor Stematsky: *Painting.* 1963. Oil. Collection the artist.

Avigdor Stematsky: *Composition*. 1963. Watercolor and pencil on paper.
Collection the artist.

Avigdor Stematsky: *Composition*.
1963. Watercolor and pencil on
paper. Collection the artist.

Avigdor Stematsky: *Painting*. 1963. Oil. Collection the artist.

Yeheskiel Streichman

Yeheskiel Streichman: *Yellow Painting*. 1963. Oil. Galerie Israel Ltd.

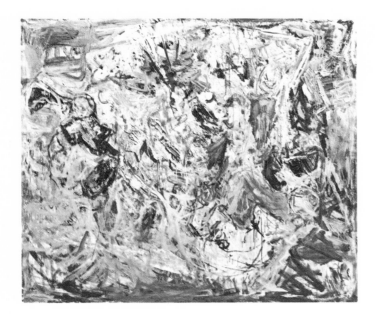

Yeheskiel Streichman: *After Poussin.* 1964. Oil. Galerie Israel Ltd.

Yeheskiel Streichman: *Abstract Painting.* 1962. Oil. Galerie Israel Ltd.

Statement by the Artist

Painting grows out of a culture as a flower out of fertile ground. Painting is a whole weltanschauung, *and does not develop very far when supported by talent alone—however rich the talent may be. I therefore believe that teaching cannot be merely a lesson in technique, but must be considered a means of conveying a message.*

I do not think that I am influenced by any particular painting, but I am bound to a tradition. My painting stems from a long European lineage—Tiepolo, Fragonard, the Nympheas *of Monet. My generation of abstract painters has been generally nourished in impressionism. My abstraction is a natural outcome of all these and of others. There is no returning: easel painting, as it is now, may disappear in the near future, but there is no way back to literary painting.*

I consider myself an Israeli painter. The physical fact of Israel is the very source of my inspiration. I witnessed the revival of the Jewish State. My painting is clear, colorful, and joyous (not to be misconstrued to mean that the painter is happy). I reject the sombre Jewish painting with its literary, religious, and philosophical symbols. I consider that the use of Jewish symbols is merely a way of exploiting sentiment. By this, I definitely affirm my Judaism. As a matter of fact, I am a Zionist painter. Israeli painting should be free, vibrant, rhythmic, and alive. I use light colors— pinks, yellows. I feel that I am an integral part in the rebuilding of Israel—not unlike a construction worker.

Tel Aviv, 1964

Moshe Tamir

71

Moshe Tamir: *Satellite*. 1963. Oil and tempera.
Collection the artist.

Statement by the Artist

Perhaps before the War of Independence, painting for me was only a matter of art and esthetics—a world of beauty that the young boy I was then wanted to conquer.

However, with the war, painting became a life itself and began to fit in within a definite framework. Friends had perished. I had to continue their lives. Life and painting blended and became one and the same.

I am not pessimistic. On the contrary, my last painting (March 1964), Lot's Wife, is —if I may say so—a condemnation of those who go on living in the past. Life— first of all! Everything I have achieved since the age of eighteen in the field of technique— whether it be oil, tempera, or fresco— has been only in order to express myself more adequately, strongly, deeply—not for the sake of technique! Life—first of all—and art only as a means of expression.

Jerusalem, 1964

LEFT: Moshe Tamir: *Lot's Wife*. 1964. Oil and tempera. Collection the artist.

FAR LEFT: Moshe Tamir: *Messenger*. 1963. Oil and tempera. Collection the artist.

Anna Ticho

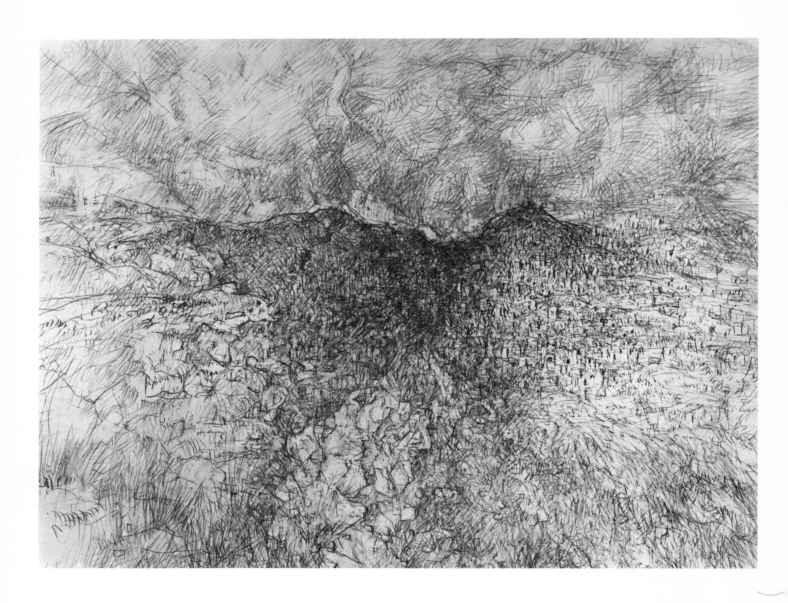

Anna Ticho: *Jerusalem: Storm*. 1963. Charcoal on paper. Collection the artist.

Anna Ticho: *Jerusalem Mountains.* 1963.
Charcoal on paper. Collection the artist.

Anna Ticho: *Jerusalem Landscape.* 1963. Pen
and ink on paper. Collection of Mrs. Elisheva
Cohen.

Statement on the Artist

The earlier drawings by Anna Ticho show many of the well-known landmarks of Jerusalem and its surroundings. In recent years, however, Anna Ticho has become more and more independent from nature. The motif as an identifiable spot has nearly disappeared. Although she still seeks inspiration in nature, the actual work is done entirely in the studio. When the first rough sketch has been put on paper in the open, a slow and lengthy process starts. Eventually the work, growing under the artist's hand, develops a will of its own and may finally ripen into something quite different from the original sketch. Anna Ticho has learned to accept that kind of guidance from her own work. It leads her away from the realistic representation of nature, but at the same time, makes her realize its essence. A breath of growth blows through the latest landscape drawings. The trees, shrubs, and mountains express nature's moods in all their variety; there is the joy of growing, but also the menace of destruction, the eternal mystery of death and rebirth.

For all of us who know and love Anna Ticho's work, these recent drawings come as a great surprise. The artist has moved in an entirely new direction. Using all the artistic experience and technical knowledge achieved during a lifetime devoted to the art of drawing, she presents us with works of a dream-like quality, creations of pure fantasy molded into form. There is, however, not a trace of idealization. This is abstraction, not in the sense of being non-objective, but of grasping and expressing the essential.

Anna Ticho's art has reached a new goal, but the road leads on, and there are no limits for the genuine artist.

Elisheva Cohen, Jerusalem, 1963

Yigael Tumarkin

LEFT: Yigael Tumarkin: *Hiroshima.* 1960. Polyvinyl chloride and iron on wood. Galerie Israel Ltd.

BELOW: Yigael Tumarkin: *Crucifixion.* 1962. Polyvinyl chloride and iron. Galerie Israel Ltd.

Statement by the Artist

It does not matter where the artistic fact starts—with bronze, canvas, rubbish . . . what matters is to create a new reality—to create order out of disorder. What matters is to break with the conventional and literal meaning and use of objects. A pagan uses a nail, a tooth, for its instrinsic beauty or magic force, for its elemental value.

I do not paint like the Renaissance or later masters out of admiration for them. I am unable to compete with them. My brush is an instrument—like a seismograph or like the crude brush of the house painter.

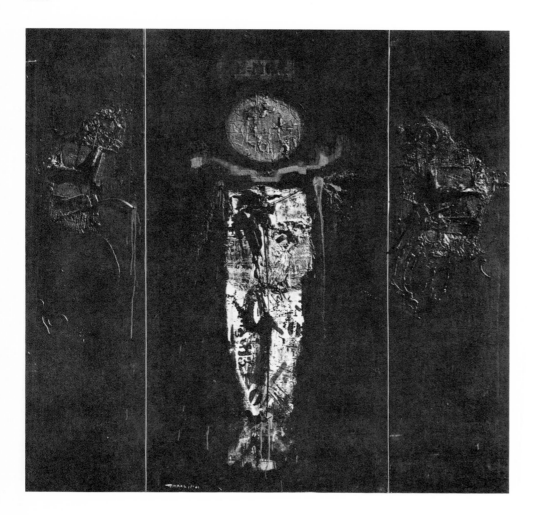

I am trying all kinds of experiments. One of the pitiable aspects of twentieth-century man is his specialization. There are people specializing in painting squares! This specialization isolates the man—separates him from society. Although I have failed in a great many of my experiments, I have learned from all of them.

Israel is a country in the process of rebuilding and in which I am at home. I am no longer the stranger I was in the Europe of the cathedral or in the America of the skyscraper. There, everything has already been done.

Unfortunately, here, as everywhere else, the present generation of "art dictators" does not distinguish between art and pure decoration; ninety percent of what is being built—gardens, structures—is decoration—not creative art.

The Mediterranean has, from the beginning, been the cradle of sculpture. Here, light changes constantly and continually alters the landscape. My dream—to build a temple of my own to these lights and landscapes.

Tel Aviv, 1964

77

LEFT: Yigael Tumarkin: *Sculpture*. 1963.
Bronze. Galerie Israel Ltd.

RIGHT: Yigael Tumarkin: *Crematorium*.
1964. Welded iron. Galerie Israel Ltd.

Yaacov Wexler

Yaacov Wexler: *Tension in Space*. 1962.
Polyvinyl chloride. Galerie Israel Ltd.

Statement by the Artist
I try to build a world of my own, governed by harmony and beauty. I shall stand up against threatening destruction and bareness.

Tel Aviv, 1964

Yosef Zaritsky

Statement on the Artist

Yosef Zaritsky occupies a very special place in Israel's world of plastic arts. His importance lies not only in his extraordinary achievements as a painter, but equally in his role as a guide and pathfinder who brought Israel within the orbit of new directions in the plastic arts. In fact, he is the spiritual father of lyric abstraction in Israel.

Zaritsky's long and consistent road, from his watercolors of the twenties to his abstract oils of today, is not adequately explained by the term "abstract impressionism," which was customarily attached to this artist.

The transference of the emotional value of shades of color to the material aspect of paint, the sensitivity, strict formal structure, and spontaneity, at one and the same time, all give proof of the fact that he has divorced himself finally from impressionism, although it constituted for him the original source of influence.

It is comparatively simple to explain the structural form of Zaritsky's works: the artist builds on a two-dimensional surface with layer upon layer of variations of forms; each layer is separated from the former by shades of color, degrees of transparency and thickness, and the strokes of his brush. All layers together combine to create a counterpoint of form, rich in expression and high inner tension.

True, this formal explanation does not suffice to explain the emotional values in-

LEFT: Yosef Zaritsky: *Painting.* 1954. Oil. Collection Mr. and Mrs. Israel Zafrir.

FAR LEFT: Yosef Zaritsky: *Amsterdam.* 1956. Oil. Collection the artist.

herent in the works of this master painter. Words are inadequate to describe the essence of the meaning of a creation that flows from a unique lyric sensitivity.

A painting of Zaritsky's demands that the viewer experience with the painter the entire process of creation, from his approach to the naked canvas until the final stroke on its surface. Only in this way can he discover the unusual emotional power coupled with intense sensitivity which satisfy the strictest demands of the most intellectual viewer.

Note on the artist by Yoav Bar-El, art critic of the newspaper *Haaretz*, Tel Aviv, 1964.

Yosef Zaritsky: *Painting*. 1964. Oil. Collection the artist.

Acknowledgments

The selection and preparation of this exhibition have been marked by many satisfactions and pleasures, and also by certain difficulties that, I am happy to say, were surmounted. Among the satisfactions was the opportunity to visit many Israeli artists, to discuss with them their works, aims, and problems, and to feel their intensity and sincerity. My work with Mrs. Berthe Kolin, Chairman, Art Committee, America-Israel Cultural Foundation, Miss Anne Kostant, Director, Women's Division, Mr. Jochanon Samuel, General Secretary, Tel Aviv, and other volunteer workers and staff members was enjoyable and enriching. That solutions were found for many problems must in large part be credited to the commitment, knowledge, and patience of Dr. Pola Eichenbaum, whose skillful assistance was constantly available to me from the first preliminary arrangements until the final collection and shipment of the exhibition. Dr. Eichenbaum also procured statements by the artists and supplied information for the biographical notes.

On behalf of the International Council of The Museum of Modern Art and the America-Israel Cultural Foundation, I wish to thank Dr. Karl Katz, Director of the Bezalel National Museum in Jerusalem, whose advice and encouragement were of great value; and, for assistance while choosing works by Israeli artists working in Paris, the Honorable Walter Eytan, Israeli Ambassador to France, and Madame Helena Rubenstein. I am also grateful to the museums, collectors, dealers, and artists who have lent works to the exhibition.

It is a pleasure to acknowledge the work of the Museum's Department of Circulating Exhibitions, headed by Mr. Waldo Rasmussen, which organized this exhibition for circulation. Thanks are particularly due the following members of the department: Miss Carol Schapiro and Mrs. Bernice Rose for their assistance in the preparation of the exhibition; Mrs. Anne Dahlgren Hecht and Miss Nadia Hermos for editing the catalogue. The Museum's Department of Publications supervised the production of the catalogue, which was designed by Mr. Joseph Bourke Del Valle of the same department.

W.C.S.

Lenders to the Exhibition

Yaacov Agam, Paris; Mordecai Ardon, Jerusalem; Avigdor Arikha, Paris; Dr. and Mrs. Benensohn-Rosefsky, New York; Naphtali Bezem, Tel Aviv; Mrs. Yardena Brown, Tel Aviv; Mrs. Elisheva Cohen, Jerusalem; Fima, Paris; Michael Gross, Ein Hod, Israel; Shamai Haber, Paris; The Joseph H. Hirshhorn Collection, New York; Lee A. Kolker, Scarsdale, New York; Kosso, Tel Aviv; Yehiel Krize, Tel Aviv; David Lan-Bar, Paris; Mr. and Mrs. Albert A. List, Byram, Connecticut; Zvi Mairovich, Haifa; Léa Nikel, Ashdod, Israel; Ezra Orion, Kibbutz Beit Alpha, Israel; Mr. and Mrs. Gidon Schocken, Zahala, Israel; Mr. and Mrs. J. H. Schwartz, Chicago; Yehiel Shemi, Kibbutz Cabri, Israel; Avigdor Stematsky, Safad, Israel; Moshe Tamir, Paris; Anna Ticho, Jerusalem; Mr. and Mrs. Israel Zafrir, Tel Aviv; Yosef Zaritsky, Tel Aviv.
Bezalel National Museum, Jerusalem; The Museum of Modern Art, New York; The Tate Gallery, London.
Galerie Karl Flinker, Paris; Galerie Israel Ltd., Tel Aviv; Lefebre Gallery, New York; Betty Parsons Gallery, New York; Rina Gallery, Jerusalem; Howard Wise Gallery, New York.
The Knesset, Jerusalem.

Itinerary of the Exhibition

1964–65

The Jewish Museum, New York, New York: December 9–January 24
The Toledo Museum of Art, Toledo, Ohio: February 19–March 19
The Contemporary Arts Center, Cincinnati, Ohio: April 2–30
Rose Art Museum, Brandeis University, Waltham, Massachusetts: May 17–June 20
The Art Institute of Chicago, Chicago, Illinois: July 22–August 22
The Detroit Institute of Arts, Detroit, Michigan: September 7–October 3
Philadelphia Museum of Art, Philadelphia, Pennsylvania: October 18–November 15
Museum or Art, Carnegie Institute, Pittsburgh, Pennsylvania: November 29–December 27

1966

The Montreal Museum of Fine Arts, Montreal, Quebec: January 10–February 7
The Art Gallery of Toronto, Toronto, Ontario: February 25–March 25
Winnipeg Art Gallery, Winnipeg, Manitoba: April 11–May 9
Seattle Art Museum, Seattle, Washington: May 30–June 27
San Francisco Museum of Art, San Francisco, California: July 11–August 14
Municipal Art Gallery, Barnsdall Park, Los Angeles, California: September 13–October 16
Portland Art Museum, Portland, Oregon: October 31–November 28

Moshe Tamir: *War Bird*. 1962. Oil and tempera. Collection the artist.

Biographies of the artists and list of works of art

Note:
An asterisk following "Palestine" indicates that the country was under British mandate at that time.
The following prizes are often referred to in the biographies:

Struck Prize. Founded in 1946 by the Municipality of Haifa in memory of a painter and engraver who lived in Haifa, Herman Struck (1876–1944). Awarded annually to the best work of a painter or sculptor shown in the Haifa and North General Artists' Association Exhibition.

Dizengoff Prize. Founded in 1936 by the Municipality of Tel Aviv–Jaffa in memory of Meir Dizengoff (1861–1936), the first mayor of Tel Aviv. The prize is awarded annually to a painter or sculptor for the best work shown in the General Exhibition of the Artists' Association in Israel.

Israel Prize. National Israel Art Award for theater, literature, music, and painting, distributed by the Ministry of Education and Culture in Jerusalem. The prize is given each year on the anniversary of Israel's independence.

In the dimensions given, height precedes width.

Yaacov Agam (Yaacov Gipstein)

Born in 1928 in Roshon-le-Zion (one of the first Zionist settlements in Palestine*). Father a rabbi. In 1947, studied at the Bezalel School of Arts and Crafts, Jerusalem, and subsequently with Siegfried Giedion in Zurich. In 1951, moved to Paris, where he works and lives. His first one-man show, the first of several in Paris, was held at the Galerie Craven in 1953. Other one-man shows include one in New York at the Doris Meltzer Gallery in 1955 and one at the Museum of Tel Aviv in 1959. Among the group shows in which Agam has participated are: Carnegie International, Pittsburgh, 1958, 1962; "I Biennale de Paris," 1959; "Movement in Art," Stedelijk Museum, Amsterdam, Moderna Museet, Stockholm, and Louisiana Museum, Humlebaek, 1961; "Modern Art of Israel," Siebu Department Store, Tokyo, and Daimaru Department Store, Osaka, 1962; and the VII Bienal, São Paulo, 1963 (received the Prize for Artistic Research, especially created for him by the jury).

Modifiable Rhythm. 1952. Oil on composition board with pivoting wood elements. 39 x 48½ x 2¼". Galerie Israel Ltd., Tel Aviv.

Spatial Relief. 1959. Oil on wood with movable metal parts. 23¼ x 47⅞ x 11⅛" (base); movable metal parts 10¼" maximum depth. Galerie Israel Ltd., Tel Aviv.

Four Themes-Counterpoint. 1959. Oil on wood. 35½ x 47¼ x 2¾". Galerie Israel Ltd., Tel Aviv.

Natural Movements. 1961. Oil on wood with metal elements and springs. 37¾ x 47½ x 3¾". Howard Wise Gallery, New York.

Diptyque Painting. 1962–63. Oil on wood. Left panel: 27 15/16 x 9 15/16"; right panel: 27 15/16 x 9 15/16". Lent by the artist, courtesy of Marlborough-Gerson Gallery, New York.

Double Metamorphoses. 1964. Oil on wood. 39¾ x 49⅝". Mr. and Mrs. J. H. Schwartz, Chicago. (New York and Chicago showings only.)

Aïka (Aïka Brown)

Born in 1915 in Tel Aviv. Family of Russian origin. Graduated from the Bezalel School of Arts and Crafts, Jerusalem, in 1957. Had first one-man show at the Rina Gallery, Jerusalem, in 1958, and the same year received the Prize of the Israeli Ministry of Education and Culture. First one-man show in Europe at Galerie Marcelle Dupuis, Paris, 1961. Beginning in 1958, participated in many group shows both in Israel and Europe, among them "Israeli Art," Musée National d'Art Moderne, Paris, 1960. From 1959 on, divided his time between Tel Aviv and Paris. Aïka was killed in a car accident September 9, 1964, in France.

Relief Composition. 1963. Plastic materials on canvas. 59⅛ x 35¾". Mrs. Yardena Brown, Tel Aviv.

Dolls I. 1964. Plastic materials with dolls on canvas. 51½ x 51⅝ x 8⅜" irreg. Mrs. Yardena Brown, Tel Aviv.

White and Black Relief. 1964. Plastic materials on canvas. 47⅜ x 47¼". Mrs. Yardena Brown, Tel Aviv.

Mordecai Ardon (Bronstein)

Born in 1896 in Tuchow, Poland, into Orthodox Hasidic family. Father a watchmaker. In 1920, enrolled at the Bauhaus in Germany and studied there until 1925 under Kandinsky, Feininger, Itten, and Klee. In 1926, studied at the Staatliche Kunstakademie, Munich, under Max Doerner. From 1929 until 1933 taught at the Berlin Art School of his former teacher, Johannes Itten. In 1933, left Germany and settled in Jerusalem, where he met the late Mordecai Narkiss, then director of the Bezalel National Museum. From 1935 until 1952, taught at the Bezalel School of Arts and Crafts, Jerusalem, becoming its director in 1940. While teaching, had among his pupils three artists included in the present exhibition—Avigdor Arikha, Naphtali Bezem, and Moshe Tamir. In 1952, was appointed Artistic Advisor to the Israeli Ministry of Education and Culture. In 1963, was awarded the Israel Prize. First one-man show was held at the Jewish Museum, New York, in 1948. Has had numerous other one-man shows, including one at the Stedelijk Museum, Amsterdam, in 1960–61, and in Israel in 1963, at the Museum of Modern Art, Haifa, Museum of Tel Aviv, Bezalel National Museum, Jerusalem, and Mishkan LeOmanut, Ein Harod. Among the group shows in which he has participated are: "Seven Painters of Israel," Institute of Contemporary Art, Boston, 1953; the XXVII and XXIX Biennales, Venice, 1954 (received UNESCO Prize), 1958; "50 Ans d'Art Moderne," Brussels World's Fair, 1958; Documenta II, Kassel, 1959; and "Israeli Art," Musée National d'Art Moderne, Paris, 1960. Lives in Jerusalem.

Missa Dura. (Triptych). 1958–60. Oil on canvas. Left panel: *The Knight*. 76⅞ x 51⅜"; center panel: *Kristallnacht*. 77 x 102⅝"; right panel: *House No. 5*. 77 x 51⅜". The Tate Gallery, London.

The Way to Jerusalem. 1962. Oil on canvas. 51¼ x 63⅛". Bezalel National Museum, Jerusalem, gift of Mrs. Katharine Sonneborn Falk. (New York showing only.)

Timepecker. 1963. Oil and tempera on canvas. 63¾ x 51⅜". Lent by the artist.

Avigdor Arikha

Born in Radauti, Rumania (now in U.S.S.R.), in 1929. Spent 1941–44 in a Nazi concentration camp, arriving in Palestine* on May 1, 1944. Worked in a kibbutz and resumed schooling. Studied at the Bezalel School of Arts and Crafts, Jerusalem, with Ardon (who is also in the present exhibition). Wounded in Israeli War of Independence, 1948. Went to Paris in 1949 and studied painting at the Ecole des Beaux-Arts. Also studied philosophy.

Returned to Jerusalem in 1951. In 1953–54, spent some time in Sweden, returning in the fall of 1954 to Paris, where he has lived and worked ever since. First one-man show was held at the Zeïra Gallery, Tel Aviv, in 1952. First European one-man show, at the Galerie Moderne, Stockholm, in 1954. Among the group shows in which he has participated are: "I Biennale de Paris," 1959; "Israeli Art," Musée Nationale d'Art Moderne, Paris, 1960; and the XXXI Biennale, Venice, 1962. Has illustrated many books published in Israel and France. Designed stained-glass windows for the Synagogue of Woonsocket, Rhode Island, in 1961–62, and a tapestry for the S.S. "Shalom," in 1963.

Incandescences. 1959. Oil on canvas. 63¾ x 51 3/16". Lent by the artist.

Informée. 1961. Oil on canvas. 57½ x 44⅞". Dr. and Mrs. Benensohn-Rosefsky, New York.

Noirs Précipités. 1963. Oil on canvas. 38 x 63 3/16". Lent by the artist.

Naphtali Bezem

Born in Essen, Germany, in 1924, into a family of Polish origin. In 1939, sent by his parents to Palestine* through Youth Aliyah. From 1943 to 1946, studied at the Bezalel School of Arts and Crafts, Jerusalem, under Ardon (also in the present exhibition), and taught there during 1946–47. From 1949 until 1951, worked in Paris. In 1957, received the Dizengoff Prize. From 1953 to 1961, had five one-man shows in Israel, both in museums and private galleries. In 1964, had a one-man show at the Gallery Laverne, New York. Among his commissions have been: a mural for the S.S. "Theodor Herzl," 1957; two murals for the Israeli Pavilion at the Brussels World's Fair, 1958; a mural for the Sheraton Hotel, Tel Aviv, 1960; two bas-reliefs for the Tel Aviv Exhibition Grounds, 1959–61; and a sculptured wall for the El-Al Headquarters, Tel Aviv, 1962. Among the group exhibitions in which Bezem has participated are: the XXVII and XXX Biennales, Venice, 1954, 1960; the VII Bienal, São Paulo, 1963; and "Peintres Israéliens," Galerie Charpentier, Paris, 1963. Lives in Tel Aviv.

Coming Back. 1960. Oil on canvas. 51¼ x 45¾". Lent by the artist.

The Common Grave. 1962. Oil on canvas. 72⅞ x 51". Lent by the artist.

Rising Figure. 1963. Oil on canvas. 51¼ x 63⅞". Lent by the artist.

Moshe Castel

Born in Jerusalem, Palestine, in 1909, into a Sephardic family which had settled in the region five centuries before. From 1927 until 1940, lived in Paris, where he attended the Académie Julien. From 1951 to 1953, lived in the United States. First one-man show was held in London in 1931; second, the following year at the Galerie Zak, Paris. Has had one-man shows at the Gallery Lefebre, New York, in 1962 and 1963. Among his commissioned works are: a mural for the Accadia Hotel, Accadia Beach, Israel, 1955; a painting for the offices of the El-Al Airlines, New York, 1955; a stained-glass window and a mural for the S.S. "Israel," 1956 and 1957; and a mural for the Churchill Auditorium, Technion, Haifa, 1958. Castel is a founder of the New Horizons Group and has often exhibited in the group's exhibitions. He has participated in many other group shows, among them: the XXIV Biennale, Venice, 1948; Carnegie International, Pittsburgh, 1952; and the V Bienal, São Paulo, 1959 (received Grand Prize of the State). Divides his time between Safed, Israel, and Paris.

Poésie de Canaan I. 1963. Pulverized basalt mixed in oil on canvas. 64 x 51⅜". The Museum of Modern Art, New York, gift of Mr. and Mrs. David Kluger.

Manuscrit de Neguev. 1964. Pulverized basalt mixed in oil on canvas. 51 x 38⅜". Galerie Karl Flinker, Paris.

Poésie de Canaan. 1964. Pulverized basalt mixed in oil on canvas. 70 x 80". Collection of the Knesset, Jerusalem, gift of Mr. and Mrs. David Kluger. Courtesy of Lefebre Gallery, New York. (New York showing only.)

Untitled. 1964. Pulverized basalt mixed in oil on canvas. 70⅛ x 79 15/16". Lefebre Gallery, New York. (Showings outside New York only.)

Itzhak Danziger

Born in 1916 in Berlin, Germany. In 1923, immigrated with his family to Palestine*. From 1929 to 1933, attended the Bezalel School of Arts and Crafts, Jerusalem. From 1934 to 1937, studied at the Slade School of Fine Arts, University of London. When he returned to Israel in 1938, began teaching sculpture in his studio in Tel Aviv. Since 1956, has taught three-dimensional design at Technion, Haifa. Is a member of the New Horizons Group and has often exhibited with them. His first one-man show was held at the Brook Street Gallery,

London, in 1949. Participated in the International Sculpture Exhibition, Middelheim Park, Antwerp, in 1959. Has executed many monuments in Israel, among them a mural for the Hebrew University, Jerusalem, in 1956. In recent years, has turned from sculpture to town planning. Has executed, with the architect Carmi, a plan for a town of 60,000 inhabitants —Kfar Ono. Lives in Tel Aviv.

Sculpture. 1959. Welded iron. 63⅛ x 33⅝ x 30". Galerie Israel Ltd., Tel Aviv.

"The Lord is my Shepherd" (Negev Sheep). 1964. Bronze. Left: 34⅛ x 76¾ x 53¾"; right: 32⅛ x 82⅞ x 38". The Joseph H. Hirshhorn Collection, New York.

Fima (Ephraïm Roetenberg)

Born in Harbin, China, in 1916, into a family of Russian origin. In 1935 the family moved to Shanghai, where Fima studied Chinese calligraphy and painting and became familiar with Chinese life and customs. Also visited Japan. From 1945 to 1949, created stage sets, and had his first one-man show at the J.R.C., Shanghai, in 1947. In 1949, immigrated to Israel, and from 1950, worked as a construction engineer building the immigrant center at Beersheba, where his first one-man show in Israel was held in 1953. Had a one-man show at the Baltimore Museum of Art in 1960 and one in London at the Roland, Browse and Del Banco Gallery in 1962. In 1954 and 1957, traveled in Europe. Has been in numerous group shows in Israel, Europe, and the United States, including the Carnegie International, Pittsburgh, 1961. Since 1961, has lived in Paris.

Village in the Mountains. 1962. Oil on canvas. 28¾ x 36¼". Lent by the artist, courtesy of Galerie Jacques Massol, Paris.

Mountain Landscape. 1963. Oil on canvas. 78¾ x 78⅞". Lent by the artist, courtesy of Galerie Jacques Massol, Paris.

Michael Gross

Born in Migdal, Palestine*, in 1920. In 1940, graduated from the Teachers' Seminary, Jerusalem. Studied architecture at Technion, Haifa, and practiced before taking up sculpture and painting. From 1951 to 1955, studied at the Ecole des Beaux-Arts in Paris under Marcel Gimond. From 1957 until 1960, taught sculpture at the Bezalel School of Arts and Crafts, Jerusalem, and since then, at the Kibbutz Art Seminary, Oranim. In 1964, received the Struck Prize. Has participated in many group exhibitions, among them: the XXX Biennale,

Venice, 1960; Carnegie International, Pittsburgh, 1961–62; and "Peintres Israéliens," Galerie Charpentier, Paris, 1963. Lives in Ein Hod, near Haifa.

Figure in Ochre. 1963. Oil on canvas. 78⅞ x 52″. Lent by the artist.

Woman in Black. 1963. Oil on canvas. 55⅜ x 35⅝″. Lent by the artist.

Plain in Blazing Sun. 1964. Oil on paper mounted on plywood. 27¾ x 39⅜″. Lent by Mr. and Mrs. Gidon Schocken, Zahala, Israel.

Slain Soldier in the Field. 1964. Oil on canvas. 31½ x 39⅜″. Lent by the artist.

Small Figure on Blue. 1964. Casein on composition board. 19¾ x 15⅞″. Lent by the artist.

Shamai Haber

Born in Lodz, Poland, in 1922. As a child, traveled throughout Europe, going to Palestine* in 1935. From 1939 to 1945, was a member of the Jewish underground, beginning his artistic activity while serving as a border guard. In 1949, went to Paris, where, after attending several art schools, he decided to work on his own. His first one-man show was held at the Stedelijk Museum, Amsterdam, in 1951. Has had many one-man shows in Europe since then. Among the group shows in which Haber has participated are the International Sculpture Exhibition, Middelheim Park, Antwerp, 1959 (received Bourdelle Prize, awarded by a jury consisting of Giacometti, Zadkine, Arp, Pevsner, Lipchitz, and Henry Moore), and "Sculpture in the City," Festival of Two Worlds, Spoleto, Italy, 1962. His commissioned works include a monumental sculpture for outside the building by Philip Johnson for the Atomic Reactor at Rehovot, Israel, 1961–62. His sculpture was also shown at the Seattle World's Fair in 1962. Is now working on town planning for the Negev. Lives in Paris.

Untitled. 1960–61. Brittany granite. 40 x 47 x 37″. Mr. and Mrs. Albert A. List, Byram, Connecticut.

Small Monument. 1962. Brittany granite. 24⅛ x 28 x 26½″. Lent by the artist.

Kosso (Kosso Eloul)

Born in Mourom, U.S.S.R., in 1920. Immigrated with his family in 1924 to Palestine*. From 1939 until 1943, studied at the Art Institute of Chicago and toured the United States. Served in the United States Navy, 1944–45. On his return to Palestine in 1946, lived at Kib-butz Ein Harod and was in the field corps of the Jewish underground until 1948. His first one-man exhibition was shown at the Tel Aviv Museum and the Bezalel National Museum, Jerusalem, in 1957. His first one-man show in Europe was held at the Galleria Topazia Alliata, Rome, in 1962. Was a member of the New Horizons Group. Among the important group exhibitions in which Kosso has participated are the XXIX Biennale, Venice, 1958, and the International Sculpture Exhibition, Middelheim Park, Antwerp, 1959. Has been a leader in the international movement of sculpture "symposiums," and has participated in several of them. His commissioned works include a bronze sculpture for the National Memorial, Jerusalem, 1961. Received the Dizengoff Prize in 1963. Lives in Tel Aviv.

Statement. 1962. Bronze. 21 x 18 x 9¾″. Lent by the artist.

Doubleself. 1962. Travertine stone. 70⅞ x 20½ x 5⅝″. Lent by Lee A. Kolker, Scarsdale, New York. (New York showing only.)

Basic. 1963. Jerusalem stone. 26¼ x 19½ x 15½″. Lent by Lee A. Kolker, Scarsdale, New York.

Altar. 1964. Jerusalem Stone. 20⅛ x 37¼ x 24½″. Lent by the artist.

Yehiel Krize

Born in Turek, Poland, in 1909. In 1924, immigrated to Palestine*. In 1934, studied painting with Zaritsky (also in the present exhibition). In Paris, 1937–38. Spent 1951 in New York. From 1960 to 1963, taught at the Avni Studio in Tel Aviv. Had the first important one-man show at the Tel Aviv Museum in 1947. His work was shown at the XXVII Biennale, Venice, 1956; the IV and VII Bienals, São Paulo, 1957, 1963; and "Peintres Israéliens," Galerie Charpentier, Paris, 1963. Lives in Tel Aviv.

Painting. 1961. Oil on canvas. 51½ x 38¼″. Lent by the artist.

Painting. 1964. Oil on canvas. 52⅜ x 78¾″. Lent by the artist.

Composition. 1964. Gouache on paper. 39⅜ x 27⅝″. Lent by the artist.

Composition. 1964. Gouache on paper. 39⅜ x 27½″. Lent by the artist.

David Lan-Bar

Born in Rava-Russkaya, Poland (now in U.S.S.R.), in 1912. Went to Paris when young. Immigrated in 1935 to Palestine*, where he studied painting with Streichman and Stematsky (both represented in the present exhibition), Arni and Miron Sima. In 1947, studied at the Hebrew University, Jerusalem. In 1948, moved to Paris, where he still lives, and studied at the Ecole des Beaux-Arts. First one-man show held at the Galerie Breteau, Paris, in 1950, was followed by a one-man show at the Tel Aviv Museum and the Museum of Modern Art, Haifa, in 1953, and by several others. Among the important group shows in which he has participated is the VI Bienal, São Paulo, 1961.

Composition 726. 1960. Oil on canvas. 51¼ x 38⅜″. Lent by the artist.

Composition 854. 1962. Oil on canvas. 45⅝ x 35″. Lent by the artist.

Composition 859. 1963. Oil on canvas. 45¾ x 35⅛″. Lent by the artist.

Raffi Lavie

Born in 1937 in Tel Aviv, Palestine*. Studied first with the academic painter Ludwig Moos, then with the sculptor Kosso, who is included in the present exhibition. Graduated from the Art Teachers' Seminary in Tel Aviv. Teaches painting and art history. Invited by the New Horizons Group to exhibit with them. Was also represented in the "III Biennale de Paris," 1963. Lives in Tel Aviv.

Painting 100. 1963. Oil and pencil on canvas. 51¼ x 51⅜″. Rina Gallery, Jerusalem.

Painting 98. 1963. Oil, pencil, and charcoal on canvas. 36⅜ x 28⅞″. Rina Gallery, Jerusalem.

Painting 95. 1963. Oil, pencil, and charcoal on canvas. 25¾ x 39⅜″. Rina Gallery, Jerusalem.

Zvi Mairovich

Born in Krosno, Poland, in 1909. As a youth, went to Berlin, where he studied at the Academie der Kunst and the High School for Jewish Studies. Left for Paris in 1933. In 1934, immigrated to Palestine* and settled in Haifa, where he still lives. Is a founder of the New Horizons Group. His first one-man show was held at the Galerie du Siècle, Paris, in 1950. His first one-man show in the United States was held at the Parma Gallery, New York, in 1956, and his first in Israel at the Museum of Modern Art, Haifa, in 1961. Has participated in many group shows, including the II and V Bienals, São Paulo, 1953, 1959, and the XXVIII, XXIX, and XXXI Biennales, Venice, 1956,

1958, and 1962. Received the Dizengoff Prize in 1942, 1951, and 1961.

Dead Sea Landscape. 1963. Oil on canvas. 19⅞ x 24⅛". Lent by the artist.
Mitzpe-Ramon Landscape. 1964. Oil on canvas. 53¼ x 67⅛". Lent by the artist.
Mitzpe-Ramon Landscape. 1964. Oil on canvas. 35½ x 47⅜". Lent by the artist.

Léa Nikel

Born in Zhitomir, Poland (now in U.S.S.R.), in 1918. Immigrated with her family in 1920 to Palestine*. Studied with Stematsky and Streichman (both represented in the present exhibition), and with Glicksberg. From 1950 to 1962, lived in Paris, spending 1963–64 in the United States. Her first one-man show, held at the Chemerinsky Gallery, Tel Aviv, in 1954, was followed by one-man shows at the Galerie Espace, Haarlem, The Netherlands, and Galerie Colette Allendy, Paris, in 1957. Has participated in group shows in Israel, Europe, and the United States, among them "Israeli Art," Musée National d'Art Moderne, Paris, 1960, and most recently, the XXXII Biennale, Venice, 1964. Lives in Ashdod, Israel.

Composition 9. 1960. Oil on canvas. 24 x 19 11/16". Mr. and Mrs. Israel Zafrir, Tel Aviv.
Composition. 1963. Oil on canvas. 29 15/16 x 19 11/16". Lent by the artist.
Composition. 1963. Oil on canvas. 26 x 21⅝". Lent by the artist.

Avshalom Okashi

Born in Rishon-le-Zion, Palestine, in 1916, into a family of Yemenite origin. As a child, worked with his grandfather, who was a goldsmith. From 1936 until 1942, was a member of Kibbutz Ayelet Hashahar. From there moved to Acre, where he still lives with his family. The first of his several one-man shows in Israel was held at the Katz Gallery, Tel Aviv, in 1955. Among the group shows in which he has participated are: Carnegie International, Pittsburgh, 1961; "Peintres Israéliens," Galerie Charpentier, Paris, 1963; and the International Guggenheim Competition, Solomon R. Guggenheim Museum, New York, 1964.

The Prayer. 1964. Polyvinyl acetate on canvas. 79⅛ x 29⅞". Galerie Israel Ltd., Tel Aviv.
Untitled No. 2. 1964. Oil and basalt on canvas. 63¾ x 51⅛". Betty Parsons Gallery, New York.

The Shouk. 1964. Polyvinyl acetate on canvas. 26 x 32". The Joseph H. Hirshhorn Collection, New York.

Ezra Orion

Born in 1934 in Kibbutz Beit Alpha, where he still lives and works. Studied painting at the Bezalel School of Arts and Crafts, Jerusalem, and with the sculptor Yaakov Lev. Started sculpting in 1955. Had first one-man show at the Mishkan LeOmanut, Ein Harod, in 1963; a second at the Museum of Modern Art, Haifa, in 1964. In 1964, was awarded a scholarship for study abroad by the America-Israel Cultural Foundation.

High Night I. 1963. Welded iron. 77¾ x 18 x 15". Lent by the artist.
High Night II. 1963. Welded iron. 74 x 14½ x 13½". Lent by the artist.

Yehiel Shemi

Born in 1922 in Haifa, Palestine*. At the age of seventeen, left home to participate in building Kibbutz Beit-HaArava on the shores of the Dead Sea. When the kibbutz was destroyed during the War of Independence, the members moved to Western Galilee and built Kibbutz Cabri, where Shemi now lives with his family. In 1949–50, traveled to Egypt, France, and Italy, and in 1958, to Italy, France, Belgium, and The Netherlands. Subsequently visited the United States, where he studied briefly under the sculptor Chaim Gross at the Art Students League. In 1954, was awarded the Dizengoff Prize. In 1955, began to make welded sculpture. From 1957 to 1960, taught at the Kibbutz Art Seminary, Oranim. From 1960 to 1962, resided in Paris. From 1955 until the present, exhibited with the New Horizons Group. His first one-man exhibition in Israel was shown at Mishkan LeOmanut, Ein Harod, the Tel Aviv Museum, and the Bezalel National Museum, Jerusalem, in 1957. His first one-man show in New York was held at the Betty Parsons Gallery in 1960. Among the group shows in which he has participated are: "Recent Acquisitions," The Museum of Modern Art, New York, 1959; International Sculpture Exhibition, Middelheim Park, Antwerp, 1959; Carnegie International, Pittsburgh, 1961; International Sculpture Exhibition, Musée Rodin, Paris, 1961; and the VI Bienal, São Paulo, 1961.

Standing I. 1963. Welded iron. 83 x 39½ x 35". Lent by the artist.

Sculpture. 1963. Welded iron. 44⅞ x 30¾ x 25¾". Lent by the artist.
Sculpture. 1963. Welded iron. 35 x 15½ x 12⅝". Lent by the artist.

Avigdor Stematsky

Born in 1908 in Odessa, Russia. Immigrated to Palestine* in 1920. Graduated from the Bezalel School of Arts and Crafts, Jerusalem. Attended various academies in Paris. Taught with Streichman (represented in the present exhibition) in Tel Aviv. Fought in Israel's War of Independence and was badly wounded. Had first one-man show at the Tel Aviv Museum in 1939; first one-man show in Europe at the Galerie Henri Beranger, Paris, in 1951. Helped found the New Horizons Group. Has received the Dizengoff Prize twice. Among the group shows in which he has participated are: the XXIV and XXVIII Biennales, Venice, 1948, 1958; the III Bienal, São Paulo, 1955; "Israeli Art," Musée National d'Art Moderne, Paris, 1960; "Modern Art of Israel," Seibu Department Store, Tokyo, and Daimaru Department Store, Osaka, 1962; and "Peintres Israéliens," Galerie Charpentier, Paris, 1963. Lives in Safad, Israel.

Painting. 1962. Oil on canvas. 38⅜ x 51¼". Lent by the artist.
Painting. 1963. Oil on canvas. 32⅛ x 25⅝". Lent by the artist.
Composition. 1963. Watercolor and pencil on paper. 39⅜ x 27½". Lent by the artist.
Composition. 1963. Watercolor and pencil on paper. 27½ x 39⅝". Lent by the artist.
Painting. 1963. Oil on canvas. 39 x 53½". Lent by the artist.

Yeheskiel Streichman

Born in Kovno, Lithuania (then part of the Russian Empire), in 1906. In 1924, went to Palestine* to study at the Bezalel School of Arts and Crafts, Jerusalem. After graduating in 1926, went to Paris and studied at the Ecole Speciale d'Architecture. Attended the Accademia di Belle Arti, Florence, from 1928 to 1931. After returning to Kovno, immigrated to Palestine* in 1936. During 1941 and 1942, lived and worked at the Kibbutz Ashdod Ya'akov. In 1945, moved to Tel Aviv, where he devoted himself to painting and teaching. Exhibited with the New Horizons Group and had his first one-man show at the Tel Aviv Museum in 1952. Among the group exhibitions in which Streichman has participated are the XXVII

Biennale, Venice, 1954, and the III Bienal, São Paulo, 1955. Received the Dizengoff Prize in 1942, 1947, and 1952. Lives in Tel Aviv.

Abstract Painting. 1962. Oil on canvas. 53¼ x 98⅝". Galerie Israel Ltd., Tel Aviv.

Yellow Painting. 1963. Oil on canvas. 51⅜ x 76⅝". Galerie Israel Ltd., Tel Aviv.

After Poussin. 1964. Oil on canvas. 56⅛ x 63⅛". Galerie Israel Ltd., Tel Aviv.

Moshe Tamir

Born in Bendery, U.S.S.R., in 1924. Immigrated with his family to Palestine* in 1932. In 1947, graduated from the Bezalel School of Arts and Crafts, Jerusalem, receiving the Struck Prize. From 1947 to 1949, fought in the Jewish underground movement and in the War of Independence, being seriously wounded in 1948. In 1949, received the Young Israeli Artists' Prize, created in honor of the dead of the War of Independence. From 1950 to 1952, studied at the Accademia di Belle Arti, Rome. The following two years, taught at the Bezalel School in Jerusalem and at the Institute for Painting and Sculpture in Tel Aviv. Since 1954, has lived and worked in Paris, except for 1961, when he was Associate Director of the Bezalel School. His first one-man exhibition was shown at the Artists' Houses in Jerusalem and Tel Aviv in 1952. Has had numerous one-man shows in Europe, the first at the Galerie Breteau, Paris, in 1957. His frescoes on the life of Christ, made for John T. Pirie, were shown at the Carson, Pirie, Scott Gallery, Chicago, and those on the story of Bacchus, made for H. Markus, Chicago, were shown at the Carson, Pirie, Scott Gallery and at the Monede Gallery, New York, in 1960. Among group shows in which Tamir has participated are the XXVII Biennale, Venice, 1954, and the VI Bienal, São Paulo, 1961 (received Graphics Prize).

War Bird. 1962. Oil and tempera on canvas. 70¼ x 27¼". Lent by the artist.

Messenger. 1963. Oil and tempera on canvas. 76⅛ x 60⅜". Lent by the artist.

Satellite. 1963. Oil and tempera on canvas. 21¾ x 18¼". Lent by the artist.

Lot's Wife. 1964. Oil and tempera on canvas. 51¼ x 38⅜". Lent by the artist.

Anna Ticho

Born in Vienna, where she spent her childhood. In 1912, immigrated to Israel. Has had one-man shows at the Passedoit Gallery, New York, 1953; Bezalel National Museum, Jerusalem, 1959; Baltimore Museum of Art, 1962; Museum of Modern Art, Haifa, 1962; Art Institute of Chicago, 1964; Boymans-van Beuningen Museum, Rotterdam, 1964. Her work was also shown at the XXVII Biennale, Venice, 1954. Lives and works in Jerusalem.

Jerusalem Landscape. 1963. Pen and ink on paper. 24⅜ x 18 15/16". From the collection of Mrs. Elisheva Cohen, Jerusalem.

Jerusalem Mountains. 1963. Charcoal on paper. 26⅞ x 19⅝". Lent by the artist.

Jerusalem: Storm. 1963. Charcoal on paper. 19⅞ x 27⅝" (irreg). Lent by the artist.

Jerusalem Hills. 1963. Charcoal on paper. 20⅜ x 27½". Lent by the artist.

Yigael Tumarkin

Born in Dresden, Germany, in 1933. Immigrated to Palestine* with his family in 1935. In 1945, studied at the Technical School in Tel Aviv. From 1952 to 1954, served in the Israeli Navy, and the latter year, lived in the Ein Hod artists' village, where he studied sculpture under Rudolph Lehmann. From 1955 to 1961, traveled in Europe and, in Berlin, met Bertold Brecht, who stimulated Tumarkin's interest in the theater. Designed sets for productions of many of Brecht's plays during 1957–58, in Germany, The Netherlands, and Israel. In 1959, had one-man shows in Hannover, Bielefeld, and Munster, Germany, and at the Galerie St. Germain in Paris. In 1961, had first one-man show in Israel at the Bezalel National Museum, Jerusalem; in 1963, a one-man show at the Osgood Gallery, New York. Among the many group shows in which he has participated are the Carnegie International, Pittsburgh, 1961, and "The Art of Assemblage," The Museum of Modern Art, New York, 1961, circulated to The Dallas Museum for Contemporary Arts and the San Francisco Museum of Art in 1962. Divides his time between Tel Aviv and Paris.

Hiroshima. 1960. Polyvinyl chloride and iron on wood. Left panel: 96⅛ x 24⅛"; center panel: 96⅛ x 48"; right panel: 96⅛ x 24⅛". Galerie Israel Ltd., Tel Aviv.

Crucifixion. 1962. Polyvinyl chloride and iron on canvas. 77 x 51⅝". Galerie Israel Ltd., Tel Aviv.

Sculpture. 1963. Bronze. 47⅛ x 20 x 16¾". Galerie Israel Ltd., Tel Aviv.

Crematorium. 1964. Welded iron. 62¾ x 44 x 30¾". Galerie Israel Ltd., Tel Aviv.

Yaacov Wexler

Born in 1912 in Libava, Latvia (then part of the Russian Empire). Studied at the Academy of Hamburg. Immigrated to Palestine* in 1935. Had first one-man show at Gallery Jonas, Jerusalem, in 1945; first one-man show in Europe at the Tokanten Gallery, Copenhagen, in 1950. Has participated in all the New Horizons Group exhibitions in Israel, the II and VI Bienals, São Paulo, 1953, 1961, and "Peintres Israéliens," Galerie Charpentier, Paris, 1963. Lives in Tel Aviv.

Tension in Space. (Triptych). 1962. Polyvinyl chloride and fabric on canvas. Left panel: 47 x 47¼"; center panel: 47¼ x 47⅛"; right panel: 47¼ x 47⅛". Galerie Israel Ltd., Tel Aviv.

Landscape. 1964. Polyvinyl chloride on canvas. 78 x 78¼". Galerie Israel Ltd., Tel Aviv.

Yosef Zaritsky

Born in Borislav, Russia, in 1891. In 1914, graduated from the Academy of Arts in Kiev. In 1923, immigrated to Palestine*, where he lived in Jerusalem. Studied in Paris from 1927 to 1929. On his return to Israel, established himself in Tel Aviv, where in 1948 he was one of the founders of the New Horizons Group. Seldom exhibits. Had first one-man show in Europe at the Stedelijk Museum, Amsterdam, in 1955. Participated in the XXIV Biennale, Venice, 1948. In 1960, was awarded the Israel Prize. Lives in Tel Aviv.

Painting. 1954. Oil on canvas. 32 x 39½". Mr. and Mrs. Israel Zafrir, Tel Aviv.

Amsterdam. 1956. Oil on canvas. 39¼ x 39¼". Lent by the artist.

Painting. 1964. Oil on canvas. 106⅝ x 161½". Lent by the artist.